Title: *FULL CIRCLE: A Devotional for Athletes*
Volume Title: *PREGAME* (Volume 1)
Written by: Coach Anthony "Diso" Paradiso & Coach Christian A. Dickinson
Foreword by: Coach Robert "Bob" G. Neff
Illustrations by: Learning Engineered LLC
Published by: Learning Engineered Publishing

Library of Congress Control Number: 2025934069
ISBN (Print Paperback): 978-1-965741-24-5

First Edition: 2025

Printed & Created in: United States of America
Text and Illustration Copyright © 2025

Learning Engineered Publishing is a division of Learning Engineered LLC and a subsidiary of Carpe Diem Unlimited Holdings, Inc.

LEARNING ENGINEERED
PUBLISHING

A COMMITMENT TO THE MISSION

Ten percent of the proceeds from this book will be donated—five percent to the **Fellowship of Christian Athletes (FCA)** and five percent to **Campus Crusade for Christ (Cru)**—to support their continued mission of integrating faith and discipleship into the lives of athletes, students, and communities around the world.

Fellowship of Christian Athletes (FCA) is dedicated to inspiring athletes and coaches to grow in their relationship with Jesus Christ and influence others through the power of sports. FCA transforms lives on and off the field by equipping leaders and fostering faith-centered communities.

Campus Crusade for Christ (Cru) is a global ministry committed to helping people know and follow Jesus. Through student-led movements, mentorship programs, and compassionate outreach, Cru empowers individuals to explore their faith and make a lasting impact in their schools, communities, and beyond.

Thank you for partnering with us to support these impactful ministries!

TABLE OF CONTENTS

DEDICATION

For my kids Anthony, Eva, Amelia, Everly, and Autumn.
I pray that you live a life that always makes Jesus smile.

—Coach Diso

For my son Caleb, may the events in your life come full
circle as they have in mine.

To my father, who taught me to recognize the voice of
the Lord.

To Coach Duggar, who was the example of living out
Colossians 3:23-24.

—Coach Dickinson

FOREWORD

T hroughout my years at Colonial High School, I served in many roles—coach, teacher, dean, and sponsor of the Fellowship of Christian Athletes (FCA). These positions gave me a front-row seat to the lives of countless students and athletes, but a few stand out in lasting and meaningful ways.

When I was asked to write the foreword for *FULL CIRCLE 360*, I felt deeply honored—because it was written by two of those remarkable young men: Coach Christian Dickinson and Coach Anthony Paradiso.

I first met Christian when he transferred from a private school to Colonial, which was one of the largest high schools in Orange County. Our paths crossed early one morning at a "See You at the Pole" prayer gathering. He came from a strong faith-based home, and it was clear from the beginning that we shared a deep belief in Christ. That common ground sparked an immediate connection.

I invited Christian to join FCA, where he became an active member and our FCA president. Over time, I got to know his family and formed a close friendship with his father—both men of strong character and unwavering faith.

After graduation, Christian attended the University of Central Florida. A few years later, he returned to Colonial—not as a student, but as a teacher, coach, and dean. We pursued our Master's degrees in Educational Leadership together and completed the program in 1996.

Christian's impact didn't stop there. He went on to serve as an assistant principal, principal, and executive director. Today, he continues to lead with innovation and purpose as the President and CEO of Learning Engineered Publishing. He has authored several books and developed resources that shape students, educators, and families across the country.

Coach Paradiso's story is equally memorable. I first met Anthony as a junior varsity quarterback in 1992. By 1994, he led our varsity team as the starting quarterback and even broke the school's passing record. He was a gifted athlete and an excellent student. I came to know his family well—wonderful people through and through.

After high school, Anthony played football at Robert Morris University before transferring to the University of South Florida, where he earned his Master's degree in education. He later returned to coaching and has built an impressive career, including 17 seasons as a head football coach. The quarterbacks and receivers he's coached hold or share nearly every passing and receiving record in the state of Florida.

Coach Paradiso's 100 career wins earned him a place in the elite Florida "100 Wins Club," a well-deserved recognition of his lasting impact on the game.

What makes this devotional especially meaningful is the bond these two men share—a bond forged through faith, football, and a deep commitment to mentoring others. When Coach Paradiso left for college, Christian gave him his personal Bible. Years later, when Coach Paradiso's son was accepted to West Point, he passed that same Bible on to him. That's the kind of full-circle legacy this book is all about.

I often think back to that morning at the flagpole, where a group of students and a coach gathered in prayer before the start of the school day. That moment planted seeds that are still bearing fruit.

FULL CIRCLE 360 is more than a devotional—it's a testimony to the impact that faith, mentorship, and community can have on a generation. Coach Dickinson and Coach Paradiso are now carrying the torch once lit by their mentors, passing it on with wisdom, heart, and purpose.

This devotional will bless coaches, athletes, and peers alike. I pray it inspires all who read it to seek a deeper relationship with Jesus, stay grounded in His truth, and lead others in the same way.

— Coach Robert G. Neff
A grateful teacher, coach, and mentor

PREFACE

I n 1984, God placed me on the grounds of Colonial High School, beginning a journey shaped by faith, mentorship, and the transformative power of His love. Little did I know that this would mark the start of relationships and lessons that would impact not only my life but also the lives of many others. That same year, I met Coach Neff—a teacher, brother in Christ, coach, mentor, colleague, and friend. Over the years, he became an anchor in my life, influencing me far beyond the confines of the football field, weight room, or classroom. His unwavering faith and genuine walk with Christ demonstrated that true strength is not just physical; it comes from an inner resilience rooted in knowing the love of Jesus.

Coach Neff's mentorship was a masterclass in servant leadership. He believed in his athletes wholeheartedly and connected with each of us on a deeply personal level. Through grueling practices, quiet moments of reflection, and shared struggles, he exemplified perseverance, faith, and love. His life embodied the gospel in action, teaching us values like hard work, accountability, humor, and a Christ-centered focus—qualities that have guided me throughout my own life and leadership journey.

The Bible reminds us, "To whom much is given, much is required." Coach Neff lived by this principle, pouring himself into others with a heart for service. Inspired by his example, I dedicated my life to giving back similarly.

1992, I met Coach Paradiso, affectionately known as "Diso." At the time, he was our JV quarterback and the Fellowship of Christian Athletes (FCA) President. Diso was a natural optimist, always seeing the "glass as half full." With a supportive family and a coaching staff that ranks among the best in high school football history, Diso was primed to thrive. And thrive he did.

As a junior, Diso embraced his role as the understudy quarterback, using the time to master the intricacies of our passing spread offense—a rare feat for a high school athlete. His dedication paid off in his senior year when he shattered the state passing record previously set by his predecessor. He went on to play college football and later returned to his roots, continuing the cycle of mentorship and giving back.

Diso's contributions to the game and the lives of countless young athletes are nothing short of legendary. As of 2025, the quarterbacks and receivers he has coached hold all of Florida's state records for passing and receiving. His humility, however, sets him apart. Diso's life exemplifies the verse from Philippians: "Humble yourselves in the sight of the Lord, and He will lift you up." Indeed, the Lord has lifted him up. A member of the elite Florida "100 Wins Club," his success is a testament to the power of faith and humility.

While researching for a leadership book, I reached out to Diso to revisit his time at Colonial High School. During our conversation, he shared a story about a Bible I had given him as a high school graduation gift, along with daily devotion slips I had encouraged him to distribute. Diso revealed that he later regifted that Bible to his son when he left for college, along with the devotionals he had created. His son, in turn, credited those items with helping him navigate his freshman year at the United States Military Academy at West Point. Hearing this, I was overwhelmed by the profound continuity of God's work. I paused, then exclaimed, "FULL CIRCLE."

Coach Neff mentored me, and together, Coach Neff and I mentored Diso. Diso has gone on to mentor over 1,000 athletes, including the one who mattered most—his own son. The Lord's hand is evident in how our stories have come full circle.

As you read this devotional, I hope these stories inspire you to reflect on the mentors and moments God has placed in your life to shape your journey. In jest, I suggested to Diso that we publish a book compiling the shared devotions explicitly tailored for athletes. That night, an image of the book cover came to me. Inspired, I got up in the middle of the night and drafted it. The next morning, I sent it to Diso. His reply was immediate: "Coach, it would be an honor to do something that could impact so many for generations. I am 100% on board."

And so, "FULL CIRCLE: A Devotional for Athletes" was born—a labor of love, faith, and leadership that we hope will inspire future generations. If you want to explore more about Coach Neff's journey, Coach Paradiso's early days, and the full story of how these leaders shaped me, you can find these accounts in my leadership book, "It's Great to Be a Grenadier: 7 Lessons in Leadership."

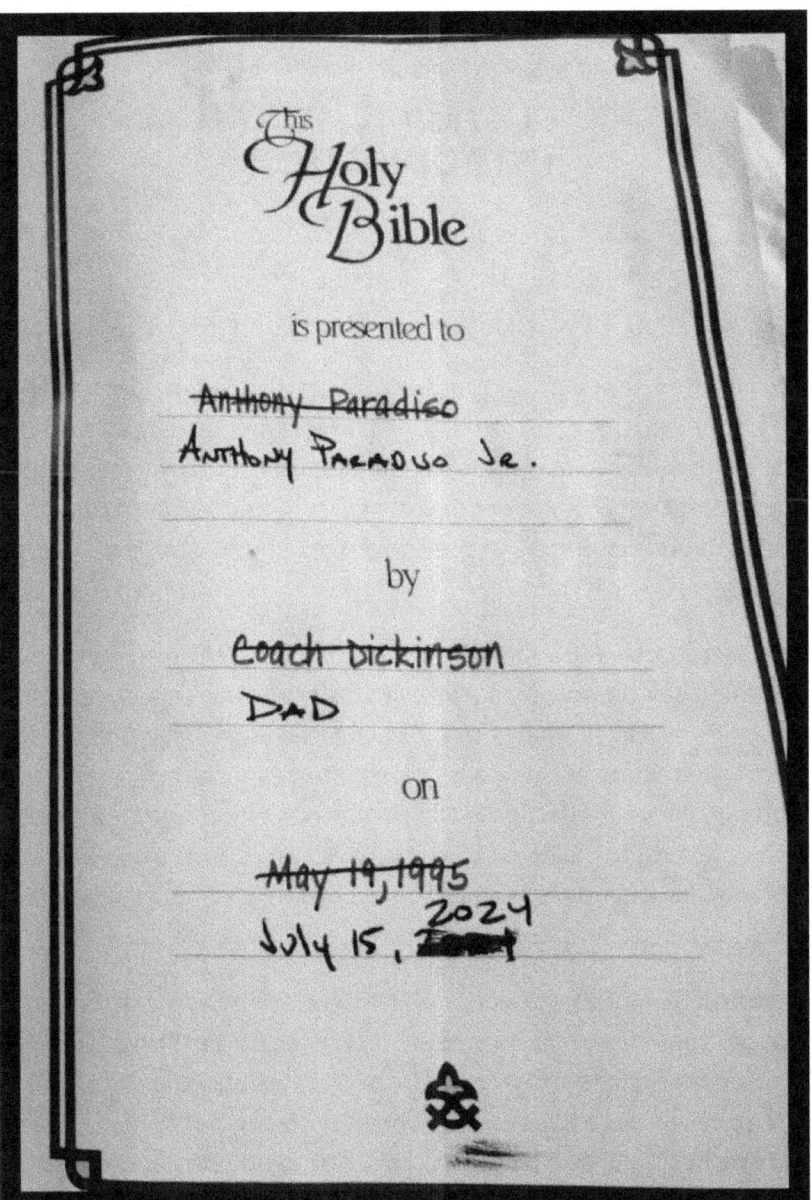

This Holy Bible

is presented to

~~Anthony Paradiso~~
ANTHONY PARADISO JR.

by

~~Coach Dickinson~~
DAD

on

~~May 19, 1995~~
July 15, 2024

INTRODUCTION

A thletes share a unique bond forged through the rigors of training, the highs of victory, the lessons of defeat, and the discipline required to pursue excellence. This bond transcends age, sport, and background, connecting current and former athletes in a shared understanding of the challenges and triumphs that come with the athletic journey.

This devotional, *FULL CIRCLE: A Devotional for Athletes*, is explicitly designed for those who have lived or are living this experience. Coach Paradiso ("Diso") and I, Coach Dickinson, have divided the devotions, sharing our own voices, stories, and insights. Occasionally, we've invited guest contributors who have been godly influences in our lives or former players to share their wisdom. These guest devotions are labeled accordingly, allowing readers to hear from broader perspectives.

The structure of this devotional is intentional. Each entry reflects the personal voice of its writer, offering you an opportunity to digest experiences and insights from coaches and players of different perspectives and ages. This diversity strengthens the message, making it robust, complete, and relevant to athletes at every stage of their faith and athletic journey.

What unites these devotions is not just our shared love of sports but our shared love of Jesus Christ. Coach Diso, our guest contributors, and I are not just Christians in name—we are followers of Jesus. Just as an athlete might follow a favorite player or team, seeking to learn all they can and emulate their example, we aim to know as much as possible about the life and teachings of Jesus. Being His disciples means striving to live out His example in every aspect of our lives, including our roles as coaches, mentors, and leaders.

This devotional is more than just a collection of thoughts; it is an invitation to walk closer to Christ while drawing upon the lessons learned through athletes' unique experiences. Whether you are stepping onto the field, reflecting on your playing days, or simply looking to grow in your faith, these devotions are here to guide, encourage, inspire, and challenge you.

So, as you journey through these devotions, may you find inspiration, divine wisdom, and a renewed sense of purpose. Just as we train our bodies to excel in competition, let us also train our hearts and minds to follow Christ with the same dedication and passion.

At the heart of this journey is the community that shaped us. For many of us, the Fellowship of Christian Athletes (FCA) was the epicenter of our faith in sports, providing a foundation that helped us navigate the game and our walk with Christ. Campus Crusade for Christ (Cru) has also played a powerful role in equipping believers to live out and share their faith boldly. To give back to these ministries that have given so much to us, 5% of all proceeds from this book will be donated to FCA and 5% to Campus Crusade for Christ.

FULL CIRCLE

A 360-DAY DEVOTIONAL FOR ATHLETES

HOW THIS BOOK WORKS

Welcome to *FULL CIRCLE: A Devotional for Athletes*!

This series is designed to inspire, challenge, and guide you on your athletic and spiritual journey. Whether you're a seasoned athlete, a coach, or someone passionate about both sports and faith, this devotional is for you.

The Series Format

The *FULL CIRCLE 360: A Devotional for Athletes* series consists of standalone books designed to encourage and equip you uniquely. While the series titles (*Pregame, Game Time, Halftime,* etc.) reflect an athlete's life rhythm, the content within is not tied to these names. Each book can be read independently, allowing you to start wherever you feel led and still experience the full impact of the message.

By design, Coach Diso and I did not collaborate on our devotions because we wrote from different perspectives. One of the most incredible aspects of the Bible—the living Word of God—is that it speaks to us in other ways at various times. As we grow, the truths we encounter deepen and mature. Similarly, hearing multiple insights on the same topic can strengthen your faith, offering unique perspectives to support your walk with Christ.

The devotions in each book were not placed in a rigid order or categorized by theme. Instead, they were arranged as they were written, allowing God to work organically through the process rather than imposing unnecessary structure. Our goal was to present these devotions as they came to us, trusting that God would use them to speak to you in His perfect timing.

The Layout

Each devotional is crafted to be concise, powerful, and practical. You can read them in any order—start wherever you feel led, and trust that God will meet you there. Here's what you can expect in every entry:

1. **Title & Theme** – Each devotional begins with a title, setting the reflection's tone.

2. **Scripture Focus** – A carefully chosen Bible verse or passage provides the foundation for the message.

3. **Reflection** – A short devotional ties the verse to real-life athletic experiences and lessons. Personal anecdotes, analogies, and practical wisdom make the truths relatable and actionable.

4. **Reflection Question** – A thought-provoking question invites you to dig deeper and apply the message to your own life, both on and off the field.

5. **Signature** – Each entry closes with Coach Diso or Coach Dickinson.

Designed for Athletes

These devotionals are written with athletes in mind but are accessible to anyone passionate about personal growth. Whether you're navigating the pressures of competition, recovering from setbacks, or seeking to balance faith and performance, these pages will serve as a source of encouragement and strength.

How to Use This Book

- **Daily Devotional** – Read one entry daily, taking time to reflect and meditate on the message.

- **Group Study** – Use the devotionals as a starting point for team discussions or small group studies.

- **On-the-Go Inspiration** – These entries are short enough to fit into your busy schedule, making it easy to stay connected to your faith wherever you are.

Our Hope

Through this series, we hope you will grow as an athlete and a person of faith, character, and perseverance. Above all, our prayer is that you will come to know the gospel of the Kingdom of God and the transformative power of Jesus Christ.

As you progress through these devotionals, may you discover new ways to live out your calling with strength, discipline, and purpose while deepening your relationship with the One who calls you to run the ultimate race.

Let's embark on this journey together. Get ready to be challenged, encouraged, and inspired as you step into the full circle of faith and athletics.

— Coach Dickinson & Coach Diso

ACKNOWLEDGEMENTS

Mrs. Morgan Champion-Dickinson

Mrs. Jessica Lynn Paradiso

Mr. Coach Rober G. Neff

Mrs. Dawn De Wulf

Mr. Coach Michael J. Duggar, Esquire

Mr. Nick Vasiliades

Mr. Joshua Ward

1

The Simplicity of God

While the Bible does not explicitly state that all of God's teachings are simple enough for a child to understand, it often conveys that faith, God's wisdom, and the path to salvation can be approached with childlike simplicity, humility, and trust. Scripture supports this idea in passages like Matthew 18:3-4, Psalm 119:130, Proverbs 1:4, 1 Corinthians 1:27, and Mark 10:15. At the same time, the Bible contains complex concepts that require context: parables meant to provoke deeper thought, prophetic writings that demand significant interpretation, and mysteries of the Creator of the universe that may remain incomprehensible on this side of Heaven.

This devotional is about the simplicity of God. Throughout Scripture, God provides straightforward commands to His people, ALWAYS tied to His greater plan. Consider His instructions to Adam:

1. Work and take care of the garden.

2. Name all the animals.

3. Don't eat from the tree of the knowledge of good and evil, or you will die.

Pretty simple commands. Yet, we know from the story that Adam and Eve disobeyed, ate from the tree, and were consequently removed from the garden and destined to die.

Or look at Noah. God told him, "Build an ark." While the command was simple, the execution was anything but. It took Noah and his family about 100 years to complete the task. Yet, their obedience ensured their survival when the flood came.

Then there was Jonah. God's instruction was clear: "Go to Nineveh." While the command was simple, Jonah's initial resistance and eventual journey revealed the complexity of carrying out God's will.

The pattern in these stories is unmistakable: God's commands are often simple in essence, but following through may involve challenges, complications, suffering, and trust. His ultimate desire is for us to obey and trust Him through the process. Two simple yet profound ideas: **Obey. Trust.**

As athletes, we're familiar with this principle. A coach's instructions during a game may be simple—"Take the shot," "Stay in position," and "Trust your teammates." But carrying them out often demands discipline, practice, and perseverance. Likewise, God's instructions may seem straightforward, but they require faith, endurance, and a willingness to rely on Him through the complexities of life.

Reflection Question

Today, reflect on the simplicity of God's commands in your life. Are you trusting Him? Are you willing to obey, even when the path forward feels challenging, or you have no idea where it might take you? Like a good coach, God's instructions are for your good and His glory—if you're willing to follow through.

— Coach Dickinson

2

The Greatest Commandment

"Jesus said, 'You shall love the Lord your God with all your heart, with all your soul, and with all your mind.'" — Matthew 22:37

Nothing is more important than loving God. This love can't just show up in the good times or only when we hit rock bottom. It can't exist only in those selfish, needy moments when we seek help. The first and greatest commandment is clear: love God with everything you are—your heart, soul, and mind.

This love must be the driving force in our daily lives, a relationship that outweighs any result. Win or lose, love God first every day. God's love is the greatest and most important thing we can experience. It surpasses the thrill of a game-winning shot, a walk-off home run, or sinking a birdie putt.

Likes, stats, championships, money, cars, clothes, or even houses—none of these replaceable things matter in the long run. What counts is on the inside. God looks at our hearts. He doesn't care about our trophies or accolades; He wants our hearts to love Him and seek a relationship with Jesus. Everything in this life is temporary, but a heart for Jesus is eternal. Always work from the inside out, letting your heart lead you to a life of love.

I want you always to pursue God's calling in your life. Whatever reason God placed you on this earth, that's what you should strive for every single day. God called me to lead my family and the teams I coached, and that purpose has lived in my heart for years. Even during moments when I felt like I failed, I never stopped trying. Your purpose is worth pursuing because it's the reason God made you.

I've struggled to see my unique gifts and talents throughout my journey. I've felt stuck or even like a failure. But in those moments, focusing on bringing others joy is essential. I feel called to help you grow closer to Jesus and to walk with Him daily. Fill your heart and your spiritual self with His love and His word. Walking with Jesus will be the greatest accomplishment of your life. Knowing He's with you in every slump will give you peace amid any storm.

Reflection Questions

1. What brings you joy in your life?

2. How could loving God first change your daily routines?

— Coach Diso

3

Go

"Trust in the Lord with all your heart; do not depend on your own understanding. Seek his will in all you do, and he will show you which path to take." — Proverbs 3:5-6

I grew up playing basketball, baseball, and soccer. I played baseball at the local Little League and participated in soccer and basketball at the small Christian school I attended. Being a mediocre athlete at a small school made collecting awards like Most Valuable Player and Most Points Scored easy. However, when I transferred to an extra-large public high school and tried out for basketball, I quickly realized I was just another player. If I were going to make an impact, I would have to adopt Larry Bird's approach—practicing more and harder than my teammates to earn playing time.

The problem was I was 5'9" at the time, and everyone else was over six feet tall except for the point guard. The point guard handled the ball like a Harlem Globetrotter, so I knew I wasn't going to take his position. Despite working as hard as I could, I realized that competitive basketball was not in my future.

Coach Neff asked me to become the Fellowship of Christian Athletes (FCA) president that same year. I accepted the role but thought, *"How in the world am I going to lead a group of athletes, Lord, when I'm not even playing a sport at school?"* The Lord put on my heart, "Go play football."

Now, I could have responded with excuses: *I've never played football. I don't know anything about football. Football is hard.* But I didn't. My father had taught me to recognize the voice of the Lord, so when He said, "Go play football," I did. I trusted Him to help me through the details of how it would play out.

That straightforward command answered my question and was the only road that would lead me to where I am today.

Athletes trust their coaches because they believe in their experience and ability to guide them to success. When a coach says, "Run this play," "Take that shot," or "Stick to the plan," athletes follow, often without hesitation. Why? Because they've spent time building a relationship with their coach, practicing under their guidance, and learning to trust their leadership.

Likewise, we should have the same level of familiarity with God. The more time we spend in prayer, studying His Word, and seeking His presence, the more we learn to trust Him when He says, "Do this" or "Go there." Just as an athlete follows a coach's lead to succeed on the field, we follow God's lead to walk in His purpose for our lives. Looking back, it's easy to see now. At the time, I could have never imagined what that choice would bring—and that's the point. The Father ALWAYS knows best. Always, always, always. Period.

We cannot see what He sees, so we trust.

Reflection Questions

1. Have you ever felt God prompting you to step outside your comfort zone? How did you respond?

2. What are some moments in your life when God's direction didn't make sense at the time but became clear later?

— Coach Dickinson

4

The Quiet One

"Blessed are the meek, for they will inherit the earth." — Matthew 5:5

Monday night's tiebreaker was upon our football team. Our opponent was the same team that had defeated us by a single point in overtime two weeks earlier. That heartbreaking loss left me, my players, and our coaching staff feeling like our chance at a championship had slipped away. I found myself wrestling with God, questioning what He was trying to teach us. How could a group of players and coaches who had given their all and acted selflessly all season endure such a tough defeat without seeing the reward for their efforts?

Before the tiebreaker game, we held a team meeting. I shared something God had placed on my heart. I reminded them of Proverbs 19:21: "Many are the plans in a person's heart, but it is the Lord's purpose that prevails." I told them that God was teaching me to reevaluate what really mattered. He didn't want me—or our team—to prioritize a championship above all else. Instead, He wanted us to put Jesus first and trust Him to take control. God calls us to live humbly, submitted to His will, so that He can lift us in His perfect timing.

As we took the field for the tiebreaker—a single quarter of play, per the rules—I told the team, "It's out of our hands, and your best is good enough for God."

The quarter started, and things weren't looking good as we struggled with field position. Our defense played tough, eventually giving us the ball back with about five minutes to go. We put together a strong offensive drive, only to turn the ball over on downs with two minutes left—just one inch short of converting on fourth down. It felt like the end, but God had other plans.

The opposing team got the ball, and what seemed like an inevitable defeat turned into a moment of divine intervention. We intercepted a pass and returned it to the twenty-yard line. With a few quick runs, we moved into field goal range and used our last timeout.

Our kicker had the chance to win the game, but his attempt missed. However, he was hit on the play, and a roughing-the-kicker penalty was called. Since our kicker was injured, he had to leave the field for one play—by rule.

That's when God reminded me of His promise: "Blessed are the meek." We sent in our backup kicker, Deighton—a young man who epitomized humility. He was always at practice, never complained about playing time, consistently encouraged his teammates, respected his coaches, and approached every moment with a smile. Deighton lined up, kicked the ball, and barely made it through the uprights—slipping just under and around four defensive players to give our school its first-ever district championship.

That night, God showed me—and our entire team—that the meek truly will inherit the earth.

Reflection Questions

1. How has God shown you that He is in control of your life?

2. What are some things you need to surrender to God and stop worrying about?

3. How does a relationship with Jesus help you overcome worry, frustration, or fear?

— Coach Diso

5

Come

Before we dive deeper into our devotional series, let's take a moment to reflect on what it truly means to be a Christian. At its core, being a Christian is about two interconnected actions: **believing** in Jesus Christ and **following** His teachings in the New Testament. Together, these define what it means to be a disciple of Jesus.

Yet, there's a distinction worth noting. Many claim the name "Christian," but not all live it out. They believe Jesus is the Son of God but stop short of actively following His teachings. I refer to these individuals as **"spectator Christians."**

Think about a sporting event. Spectators watch the game, sometimes with great enthusiasm. They may know the rules, the strategies, and even the players better than anyone else. Some are die-hard fans, fully invested in the team's success. But no matter how passionate or knowledgeable they are, they are not actually **in the game.** They have not committed to training, practicing, or stepping onto the field.

Likewise, many "spectator Christians" watch from the sidelines. They admire Jesus, believe in His divinity, and even cheer on His followers, but they haven't taken that step of full commitment—to **play the game**, to **follow Him wholeheartedly**, and to **live out His teachings** in their daily lives.

Jesus calls us to more than belief. He invites us to **come**, to **follow Him**, and to become participants, not just spectators. In Matthew 4:19, Jesus says, *"Follow me, and I will make you fishers of men."* He doesn't say, "Watch me," or "Cheer me on." He says, "Follow." This invitation requires action. It's a call to leave the stands, step onto the field, and live as His disciple.

The challenge for all of us is this: Are we content being spectators, or are we ready to **come** and follow? Are we fans, or are we disciples? Jesus is calling—**have you answered the call, or are you ready to answer?**

Reflection Questions

1. How do you define what it means to follow Jesus in your own life?

2. How might you act as a spectator rather than a disciple?

3. What steps can you take this week to actively follow Jesus and live out His teachings?

— Coach Dickinson

6

Counting the Cost

"Suppose one of you wants to build a tower. Won't you first sit down and estimate the cost to see if you have enough money to complete it?"— Luke 14:28–30

Following Jesus comes with challenges. Like an athlete preparing for competition, discipleship demands dedication, discipline, and sacrifice. Being a disciple means embracing the sacrifices and changes needed to align with Christ'steachings.

Think about stepping into the gym, eyeing the weights, or lacing up your running shoes. Often, before starting, you already know the workout will demand time, energy, and endurance. Similarly, following Jesus requires leaving your comfort zone and overcoming obstacles.

The Cost of Comfort

Every athlete knows growth doesn't happen in the comfort zone. Waking up early, pushing through soreness, or sticking to a diet are sacrifices for success. Faith challenges us to prioritize Christ's calling over convenience.

Consider the rich young ruler in *Matthew 19:21–22*. He wanted to follow Jesus but wouldn't give up his possessions. He chose comfort over commitment and missed out on greater rewards.

Are you willing to forgive, serve, or stand firm in your beliefs—even when it's uncomfortable?

The Cost of Relationships

Athletes often miss social events or downtime with friends to stay focused. Similarly, following Jesus may mean letting go of relationships or situations that pull you away from Him. Jesus said in *Matthew 10:37, "Anyone who loves their father or mother more than me is not worthy of me."*

This doesn't mean neglecting loved ones but putting Christ first—even if others don't understand.

Personally, I've missed parties and social gatherings—not because I didn't want to go, but because I wasn't invited. At first, that stung. But I realized I wasn't missing anything of lasting value over time. The reward of walking with Christ outweighed the sting of rejection. Prioritizing Him meant peace, even when people didn't get it.

Are you willing to release any relationship that competes with your devotion to Jesus?

The Cost of Reputation

You'll face critics when pursuing a goal—whether a championship or a closer walk with Jesus. Some won't understand your choices or values. Discipleship means standing firm, even when it's unpopular.

Are you willing to face criticism or rejection for Jesus?

The approval of others is fleeting, but God's approval lasts forever.

While discipleship's cost seems high, its rewards are greater. Jesus promises in *Matthew 16:25, "For whoever wants to save their life will lose it, but whoever loses their life for me will find it."*

Just as an athlete feels satisfied after months of sacrifice, we find fulfillment in committing to Jesus. The rewards—peace, purpose, and eternal life—far outweigh the costs.

Reflection Questions

1. What's one area where Jesus is asking you to count the cost?

2. What steps can you take this week to embrace discipleship's challenges with joy?

Keep training, trusting, and following the One who calls you to greatness.

Are you ready to count the cost and step into the life God has for you?

— Coach Dickinson

7

Pray for Perfect Practice

"Rejoice always, pray continually, give thanks in all circumstances" — 1 Thessalonians 5:16-18

Practice is an essential foundation of development. No matter what you're practicing for, practice will advance future results. Athletes devote astonishing amounts of time to training, traveling, and fueling their bodies. We devote so much time to the sports we love, but is our life not more important?

Why Pray?

Prayer is not a result or a habit but a relationship. Just like practice is our direct line to improving our skills; prayer expresses a real, living relationship with God. True prayer flows from a heart that desires connection with its Creator. It's not about saying the right words but about being present with the One who knows and loves us fully. Prayer deepens our intimacy with God, not because we're checking a box, but because we long to be near Him. Practice helps align our skills to our sports, prayer aligns our hearts with

His will. Our faith grows stronger as we speak, listen, and rest in His presence.

Scripture encourages us in **1 Thessalonians 5:17**, *"Pray without ceasing."* Don't look for answers from prayer; look at it as an on-going relationship with our closest friend, Jesus. Prayer is a de-pendency on God while practicing for His team. We should look at prayer as us on one knee, talking to our coach (God) during a timeout. He is our Father, and He just wants us to come to Him, sit with Him, share our days, and spend time with Him daily. Practice is a devotion and a habit towards wanting to progress, while prayer is a dependent relationship with God in which we connect to Him to advance our faith. We should be excited about the presence of God just as we would be excited to see the results of our practice sessions. Prayer fills our gas tank and hydrates our bodies with Jesus instead of a sports drink. Prayer is to walk with Jesus. To walk with Jesus, we must start with the foot of prayer, not the foot of work or accomplishments as a person or athlete.

Prayer must come first so we don't stumble. The most impor-tant step of prayer is actual prayer. Let prayer lead everything. Prayer aligns us with God first. The first step in winning anything is prayer.

"Coaches have told athletes for years that practice doesn't make perfect; perfect practice makes perfect; however, I am telling you today, prayer first, perfect practice second.

Reflection Questions

1. How can you incorporate more prayer throughout your day?

2. What benefits would prayer bring you?

— Coach Diso

8

The Foundation of Faith

"Now faith is confidence in what we hope for and assurance about what we do not see." — Hebrews 11:1

Every great athlete starts with a foundation—technique, training, and trust in the process. Similarly, our faith must be built on something solid. Without a strong base, we won't be able to withstand life's pressures or carry the weight of the calling God has placed on us.

When I first started lifting weights, I struggled to see any results. I was showing up and doing the work, but nothing seemed to change. My muscles didn't grow, my strength didn't increase, and my confidence started to dip. Still, I kept going. I had seen others make progress, and my coaches kept reminding me, "The gains come later. First, you build your base."

That stuck with me. I realized that you must trust the unseen work happening inside before you ever see the visible results—the muscles, the personal bests, the wins. Ligaments are strengthening, tendons are adapting, and foundations are being laid.

It's the same with our faith. Sometimes, it feels like we're doing everything right—praying, reading Scripture, staying consistent—but we're not seeing the breakthrough we hoped for. That doesn't mean God's not working. Like a hidden muscle being built underneath the surface, our faith is growing stronger with every rep of trust.

Jesus talked about this in Matthew 7:24–25 when He said, "Everyone who hears these words of mine and puts them into practice is like a wise man who built his house on the rock... The rain came down, the streams rose, and the winds blew and beat against that house, yet it did not fall because it had its foundation on the rock."

A house without a solid foundation might look good for a little while, but storms will eventually come. The same is true for our spiritual lives. If our faith isn't rooted in God's truth, it'll crumble under pressure.

Building a foundation of faith takes time. There are no shortcuts—just like physical training. But our spiritual strength grows when we keep showing up, trusting God's promises, and staying grounded in His Word.

You may not see the results today. But trust this: God is working. And in time, your foundation will support more than you ever imagined.

Reflection Questions

1. What are some areas in your life where you struggle to see progress?

2. How can you build a stronger foundation of faith by trusting God's promises?

3. Who has inspired your faith, and what lessons can you learn from them?

Keep training. Keep trusting. The foundation you're building now will hold up when the storms hit and carry you further than you thought possible.

— Coach Dickinson

9

Ask Big

"How much more will your Father in heaven give good gifts to those who ask him?" — Matthew 7:11

How many times do you question playing time? How many situations have you been in where you wanted to question your coach about a decision or ask for something? Over the years, many athletes have walked into my office asking questions or requesting a specific jersey number 8. The number 8 has been a Jersey number reserved for only the starting QB on the teams I coached.

Many years ago, the first young man to receive that Jersey didn't even know the legacy he was creating. At that time, Jonathan was in his first year of varsity football and had just transitioned from defense at the youth level to QB. We developed a lifelong relationship to this day; I remember this 15-year-old not knowing what jersey to wear now that he wasn't playing defensive end anymore. I recall asking him who his favorite baseball player was to help prompt his decision.

During my youth, my favorite number was 3 for Babe Ruth. I shared that with him, and he asked me what number I wore when I played QB. I told him it was 8, and he asked for that number 8 jersey. The rest is history because every quarterback I have had since then has worn that number 8 jersey. It became a great gift to receive from any player after Jonathan asked for it years ago.

God wants nothing more than to give and reward us with all we want. Just like I rewarded Jonathan's request for the number 8 jersey and how many coaches want to reward hard work and great attitudes with playing time, God wants to give us everything we ask for. God wants to do the same thing with us being His kids; however, just like a parent or coach won't reward laziness, God won't give us the things we want that will pull us away from Him.

He seeks a personal relationship with us daily in prayer, and He will give us the things He elects us to have in His time. He has already given us everything we need by offering up His Son, Jesus, to save us, but He wants us to approach Him daily and ask big with the right heart and a life centered on Him; he will always give us what we ask for according to His will if we remain faithful to Him.

There may be moments when things don't turn out how we hoped, like when I wanted Jonathan to wear number 3. But if we continue to trust Him through it all, the blessings He has in store for us are far greater than anything we could ever imagine.

Reflection Questions

1. Is there something you desire right now (like playing time, recognition, or success) that might be more about personal gain than God's purpose for my life?

2. Can I think of a time when God's plan turned out better than

what I originally wanted?

10

Fruit of the Spirit: LOVE

"And now these three remain: faith, hope, and love. But the greatest of these is love." — 1 Corinthians 13:13

In sports, as in life, love goes beyond emotions—it's about action. Christ demonstrated love by serving others selflessly. As an athlete, you have daily opportunities to show love through acts of kindness, encouragement, and putting the needs of your teammates—or even your opponents—ahead of your own. Love isn't just a feeling; it's a choice and daily actions reflecting Christ's love.

Paul's words in 1 Corinthians 13 remind us that love is the cornerstone of our faith. While faith inspires us to trust God and hope sustains us through challenges, love sets us apart as followers of Christ. It's an active reflection of His character and a powerful testimony to the world. In sports, love transforms competition into an opportunity to honor God through selflessness and grace.

During my senior year, we had a weightlifting match. I noticed a new lifter from the opposing team in my weight class. He was inexperienced, and during his first lift, he struggled with the technique and looked like he wanted to give up.

Our coach always encouraged us to start with an easy lift to get on the board, so I followed that advice. After my opening lift, I watched my competitor attempt his second lift. It was still below my opener, but he managed to complete it successfully. By his third lift, he finally surpassed my initial lift. That's when I saw an opportunity to show some love.

I asked my coach if I needed to win my class for the meet. When he said it wasn't necessary, I asked if I could attempt a new personal max, and he agreed. I went for the heavier weight on my second and third attempts but failed both times. It wasn't that I hadn't tried—I simply wasn't mentally or physically prepared for a new max that day.

I allowed my competitor to win his weight class by missing my final lift. The look on his face said it all—it was his first win, and it meant the world to him. My coach never knew what I had done, and I never told anyone. It was a small way to put someone else's desires before mine and take a back seat when it wouldn't hurt the rest of my team.

That small moment taught me that a trophy or scoreboard doesn't always measure true victory. Putting someone else's needs first reminded me of Christ's call to love others as He loves us. That moment strengthened my understanding of what it means to lead with love.

As an athlete, love can be as simple as cheering on a teammate having a bad day or helping an opponent recover after a tough loss. These small acts show that your identity is rooted in Christ, not just your field performance.

In sports and in life, love is lived out through selfless choices. Just as Jesus put us first, we're called to put others first—even when it costs us the win. That's how we reflect Christ's love and become true leaders.

Reflection Question

How can you reflect Christ's love on and off the field today?

— Coach Dickinson

11

Given Not Earned

"A new command I give you, that you love one another just as I have loved you, you also must love one another" — John 13:34

Love is rarely earned or deserved. It is a gift we choose to give, sometimes even when we don't want to. We must not let pride get in the way. We need to learn to love as God loves. Others should see the love of Jesus in us through the way we demonstrate love.

During my high school playing days, I tried my hardest to earn my father's love through performance. My "Pops" was a hardworking man who did whatever he could to provide for our family. He worked countless hours and rarely had time to take me to or attend practices and school functions or spend time with me on the weekends. Pops had only one day off each week—Sundays—and he chose to spend that day at the ball field, throwing me BP. I cherished that time with my dad.

My dad made sports an idol, and when I transitioned to high school, that priority didn't change. He never missed a Friday night football game.

Chasing my dad's love motivated me to practice harder, hoping my performance on the field would make him proud or love me more. However, I became bitter as I grew older and saw him engage with, encourage, and love my son. I wondered, *Why didn't I deserve that kind of love?*

After much prayer and reflection, I realized that "Pops" did love me. God revealed this to me through the relationship I observed between my dad and his grandson. It came full circle, teaching me to love my father as God loves me.

We must show gratitude through our relationships—with parents, friends, colleagues, spouses, or children. Honor them. Show patience and grace. Listen with love. Let them see the love of Jesus through your actions.

After much prayer and reflection, I realized that "Pops" did love me. God revealed this to me through the relationship I observed Between my dad and his grandson. It came full circle, teaching me to love my father as God loves me. We must show gratitude through our relationships—with parents, friends, colleagues, spouses, or children. Honor them. Show patience and grace. Listen with love. Let them see the love of Jesus through your actions. I've come to love "Pops" with no conditions, no expectations—just love. And in that, something beautiful happened. Our relationship shifted from me striving to earn his love to a place where every conversation is filled with warmth, understanding, and a deep, shared love that continues to grow. Throughout my coaching career, I've witnessed many athletes striving to earn love, prove their worth, or gain status through performance. Don't let positive or negative outcomes determine your love for others. God's love is unconditional.

Reflection Questions

1. Are there people in your life you've been loving based on performance?

2. How can you reflect God's unconditional love in your relationships today?

— Coach Diso

12

Fruit of the Spirit: JOY

"The joy of the Lord is your strength." — Nehemiah 8:10

J oy, as described in this verse, was one of Coach Neff's favorite principles. He created a Fellowship of Christian Athletes (FCA) group around this truth and hung the verse in the weight room, where it stayed throughout my high school and professional career at Colonial. It was a constant reminder that joy rooted in Christ doesn't depend on the scoreboard—it comes from knowing your identity in Him.

Joy isn't about ignoring challenges or pretending everything is perfect in sports. It's about anchoring yourself in Christ's unchanging love and purpose. Some joy is loud—like a game-winning shot. But the deepest joy is steady, even in the ups and downs of competition.

"The joy of the Lord is your strength." — Nehemiah 8:10

Sometimes, sharing in someone else's joy can be one of the toughest challenges. It's easy for envy to creep in when the enemy whispers lies like, *"You're not good enough,"* or *"They didn't deserve that win."* But those are lies. Joy in Christ frees us to celebrate others' success because our identity isn't tied to outcomes.

For me, embracing this truth changed everything. When someone else outperformed me, I learned not to view it as my failure but as an opportunity to grow. Their victory became a benchmark to aim for—a challenge to push myself harder. That's what I love most about sports: **accountability starts with yourself.** Before blaming refs, coaches, teammates, or bad luck, we must look in the mirror and ask, *"Did I give everything I had?"* Owning your performance—good or bad—is how you grow.

Sometimes, the hardest truth to accept is this: your best might not be enough to win. And that's okay. Good days and bad days are part of the journey. But when we let the joy of the Lord strengthen us, we find meaning in both the struggle and the success.

That's a joy that lasts.

That's joy not built on fleeting victories but rooted in Christ.

Reflection Question

1. How can you let the joy of the Lord strengthen you in both success and struggle?

2. When someone else wins, how can you choose to celebrate rather than compare?

— Coach Dickinson

13

Grateful for God

"Give thanks in all circumstances; for this is God's will for you in Christ Jesus." — 1 Thessalonians 5:18

There's something powerful about the end of a sports season. Whether it ends with a trophy or a tough loss, it's a moment to pause and reflect. Award ceremonies—like the ESPYs or even your school's end-of-season banquet—are full of highlights, emotions, and gratitude. Athletes step up to the mic and say things like, "First, I want to thank God," or "I couldn't have done this without my teammates and coaches." That moment of thanks? It's bigger than a speech. It's a window into what matters most.

But here's the deal—gratitude isn't just for award ceremonies or big wins. It's a lifestyle. And if you're following Jesus, it's non-negotiable. Paul says it clearly: *"Give thanks in all circumstances."* Not *some.* Not just when things are going your way. *All.*

When we truly give thanks—especially to God—three things start to shift in us.

First, our trust in God grows. When you take a second to remember what God's already done—how He showed up in that hard moment, gave you peace when you were anxious, or opened a door you didn't see coming—it strengthens your faith for what's next. We forget fast, but gratitude helps us hit rewind and remember He's always been faithful.

Second, we shape our mindset with faith instead of fear. Do you want to walk into your next game, challenge, or decision with confidence? Start with thankfulness. It reminds you that the same God who carried you before will carry you again. Gratitude trains your heart to expect His goodness—not just react to circumstances.

Third, we pass it on. People are watching—your teammates, younger athletes, even your family. When you live with real, consistent gratitude, you show others what it looks like to walk with God. That legacy? It's bigger than any championship banner. You're planting seeds in others that could grow into lifelong faith.

At the end of the day, I am who I am because of God. Period. Every blessing, every opportunity, every second of strength—it all comes from Him. And His greatest gift? Jesus. The ultimate sacrifice so we could have life. That's why I'm thankful. Not just when I win. Not just when things feel good. But always.

So let's be athletes who live it—on and off the field. Grateful hearts. Eyes on Jesus.

Reflection Question

How can you model gratitude toward God in a way that positively impacts those around you, especially future generations?

— Coach Diso

14

Fruit of the Spirit: PATIENCE

"Wait for the Lord; be strong and take heart and wait for the Lord." — Psalm 27:14

P atience is about trusting God's timing—whether healing from an injury, developing a skill, or waiting for a breakthrough. But this trust isn't passive; it's an active choice to grow in patience with yourself and others.

Patience shows up in two ways: how we treat ourselves and how we treat others. Some people find it easy to extend grace to others but struggle to be kind to themselves. Others are patient with their progress but quickly grow frustrated with those around them. Recognizing where you need growth is the first step.

I remember one athlete—Sam—who tore his ACL his junior year. Rehab was grueling. At first, he was all in. But around month four, frustration crept in. He started skipping smaller exercises and jumped into light lifting before he was cleared. It cost him. He reinjured his knee during a casual pickup game, setting him back several months. It was a hard lesson in the cost of impatience. On the flip side, I've seen athletes who stick with the process—trusting their trainers, listening to their bodies, and staying consistent—come back stronger than ever.

If patience with yourself is a struggle, start by setting realistic expectations. Surround yourself with people who encourage you and remind you how far you've come. If patience with others is difficult, ask where pride might be creeping in. Impatience often grows from believing that we could do something better or faster—a mindset humility can help correct. Remember, waiting on the Lord strengthens us to show grace to ourselves and others.

Reflection Questions

Where in your athletic journey must you trust God's timing instead of rushing the process?

Who in your life is God calling you to be more patient with this week?

— Coach Dickinson

15

Control

"The mind governed by the flesh is death, but the mind governed by the Spirit is life and peace." — Romans 8:6

In sports—and in life—there are things we can control and things we can't. I've seen it firsthand countless times. One athlete stands out in my memory—a young man with incredible potential who fractured his femur during his sophomore season. It was a tough break, literally and figuratively. After surgery and a long road of rehab, he missed his entire junior season. The physical recovery was hard, but the mental battle was even harder. He lost confidence, consumed by fear that his leg might fail him again.

That experience taught me an important lesson: uncontrollable events will always come our way. The question is, how do we respond? Do we let fear take over, or do we hand those uncontrollables over to God? Faith is the key. Without it, we're left spinning in uncertainty. When we thank God in advance for His plan, we're not only expressing our trust in Him—we're also reminding our hearts of His deep love, faithfulness, and care for us. Gratitude shifts our focus from what we lack to what God has already promised.

It invites peace into our present and hope into our future. *"Do not be anxious about anything, but in every situation, by prayer and petition, with thanksgiving, present your requests to God." – Philippians 4:6 (NIV).*

When we try to navigate life without trusting God, doubt creeps in. That doubt brings fear, and fear can lead us down a destructive path. It clouds our decisions and robs us of the peace we can find through faith. But when we let go and align our hearts with God, something incredible happens—He gives us strength and clarity, even in the hardest moments.

That young man? He didn't let fear win. He leaned on his faith, worked hard, and returned to the field his senior year. Not only did he help lead his team to the playoffs, but he was also named "Team MVP." While not every situation will have the same outcome, one thing is certain: God will always be by our side. No matter what, we can choose faith and trust Him with every part of our lives.

While not every situation will have the outcome we hope for, one thing remains certain: God will always be by our side. The ending may not always look like a victory, and our faith will be tested, but we have a choice in every moment. We can choose faith. We can choose to trust Him with every part of our lives, even the uncertain, painful, or unfinished parts. Faith doesn't erase the unknown but brings peace in the middle of it by shifting our eyes from the chaos around us to the character of Jesus —His goodness, faithfulness, and promises.

Reflection Questions

1. What setbacks have you faced that tested your faith?

2. What's one area of your life you can give up control and

trust God with today?

— Coach Diso

16

Fruit of the Spirit: PEACE

"Peace I leave with you; my peace I give you. I do not give to you as the world gives. Do not let your hearts be troubled and do not be afraid." — John 14:27

Christ's peace calms our hearts in the face of pressure and uncertainty, reminding us that He is in control.

In high school, I became the field goal kicker almost by default. I had grown up playing soccer, so I knew how to strike a ball cleanly—and I didn't need a steel-toed shoe. But unlike soccer, where kicking is routine, kicking a field goal in football comes with intense pressure. All eyes are on you. The outcome often rides on your ability to block out the noise, settle your nerves, and deliver.

It was my senior year, and we were playing the homecoming game. Coach Neff called my name and asked, "Can you make a kick from that far?"

I hadn't been asked to kick from that distance before—but I looked at the ball, placed it on the right hash, and said, "I like the right hash." After a quick pause, I confidently answered, "I can make it."

The head coach looked at Coach Neff and asked, "Can he really make it?" Without hesitation, Coach Neff said, "He can make it." Then he grabbed my helmet, leaned in, and said through my earhole, "You got this," before giving me a push onto the field.

Jogging out, I felt an incredible sense of peace rush over me—something I'd never experienced before in a game. I knew I had the leg strength, but the weight of the moment had me questioning myself. Yet Coach Neff's belief in me, paired with a quick prayer as I glanced toward the sky and whispered, "Lord, help me," filled me with a peace that defied logic.

The nod from the holder sealed it. The snap came, I stepped through and kicked a 43-yard field goal. It sailed through the uprights. Coach yelled, "You did it!"

The peace I felt in that moment wasn't confidence. It wasn't swagger. It was something deeper. It was divine. It was supernatural.

Reflection Question

How can you invite Christ's peace into the pressures of your sport or life?

— Coach Dickinson

17

Real Confidence

"Let us then approach God's throne of grace with confidence." — Hebrews 4:16

Throughout my journey as an athlete and coach, I've seen the transformative power of real confidence. It's the kind of confidence that uplifts individuals and inspires entire teams. Genuine confidence isn't about how you measure up to others or chasing external validation. Instead, it comes from a deep understanding of who you are and where your worth truly lies.

Too often, people think confidence is tied to pride, talent, or results. Success can be fulfilling, but if your confidence relies solely on winning, it becomes fragile. Everything you've built can crumble when failure hits—and it will.

Over time, I've learned that true confidence isn't rooted in personal achievements. It's rooted in something far greater than ourselves. For me, that foundation is Jesus. When you trust something eternal, you gain the freedom to grow, fail, and learn without fearing losing your identity. You no longer need to pretend you've got it all together. Hebrews 4:16 challenges us to approach God's throne with confidence. That verse has become a guiding principle in my life. Whether standing in the batter's box or lining up a crucial putt, I know I'm not alone. My confidence doesn't come from my abilities or the scoreboard; it comes from knowing that God's grace surrounds me—win or lose. Success is worth celebrating in sports and life, but it can't be our only source of strength. Instead, let's anchor ourselves in something timeless. When we step onto the field or court, let's do it with the unshakable knowledge that we are loved, guided, and never alone. With that kind of confidence, we can face any challenge—and inspire others to do the same.

Reflection Questions

1. Think back to a moment when you felt truly confident and successful. What made you feel that way?

2. How can placing your confidence in Jesus reshape how you approach tough situations?

— Coach Diso

18

Fruit of the Spirit: KINDNESS

"Therefore, as God's chosen people, holy and dearly loved, clothe yourselves with compassion, kindness, humility, gentleness, and patience." — Colossians 3:12

K indness reaches the heart of Christ and uplifts others in ways nothing else can. It's not weakness—it's strength under control. Kindness is a mindset that flows from a heart transformed by Jesus.

For athletes, kindness shows up in the smallest moments: offering a hand to help an opponent up after a tough play, encouraging a teammate after a mistake, and respecting a coach's decision even when you disagree. One of our former opponents was injured during a playoff game, and our team helped carry him to the sideline. That act of kindness transcended the competition. It changed the game's atmosphere and reminded everyone that sportsmanship matters more than stats.

That reminded me of the way Jesus treated others. He didn't just heal people's bodies—He noticed their hearts. Whether calming storms, feeding crowds, or gently correcting sin, Jesus led with kindness. His kindness softened hearts and transformed lives.

Practicing kindness doesn't mean lowering your intensity, goals, or grit. I've seen some of the toughest athletes lead with kindness—bringing energy to the locker room, hyping up younger players, and ensuring no one gets left behind. That's the kind of leader people want to follow.

Kindness means choosing to overflow with the heart of Christ: showing up, being present, and lifting others up. It inspires teammates, builds friendships, and strengthens team culture in ways that talent alone never could.

Kindness doesn't make you soft. It makes you someone people can count on—because you reflect the grace of Christ.

Reflection Question

What opportunity do you have this week to show kindness in a high-pressure moment—on your team, in your friendships, or during competition?

— Coach Dickinson

19

G.O.A.T.

"I press on toward the goal to win the prize for which God has called me heavenward in Christ Jesus." — Philippians 3:14

The term *G.O.A.T.* is thrown around a lot these days, standing for the "Greatest of All Time." It sparks countless debates—Michael Jordan or LeBron James? Growing up, Michael Jordan was *the* guy. He wasn't just a player; he was a phenomenon. Everyone wanted to "Be Like Mike." We'd watch his every move, lace up our Air Jordans, and try (and fail) to mimic his dunks on the driveway hoop.

Now, LeBron has built his legacy, redefining what's possible as he continues to dominate the game well into his forties. These players set the bar so high that they inspire generations to aim for greatness.

Sports icons like MJ or LeBron give us a blueprint—a vision of what hard work, perseverance, and dedication can achieve. They show us what's possible if we put in the time and effort. But here's the thing: as much as we admire these legends, we must remember they're human, not divine. Icons can inspire us, but they should never become idols.

It's one thing to say, "I want to be like Mike," and another to let that admiration morph into, "I want to *be* Mike." When we start idolizing people—whether it's athletes, celebrities, or anyone else—we lose sight of who God created us to be. Philippians 3:14 reminds us to keep pressing toward the ultimate goal: the life God has called us to in Christ Jesus.

Admiring greatness isn't wrong. It can motivate us to be better. But we need to keep our priorities straight. There's only one King, and it's not King James or anyone else. Our identity and purpose must always be anchored in God.

So, let MJ or LeBron inspire you to work hard and chase excellence. Let them be reminders that greatness is within reach when you give your all. But never forget: your worth isn't measured by stats or highlight reels. It's found in your relationship with Christ and your unique gifts and calling. The true G.O.A.T. isn't found on a court or field—it's Jesus, and He's the one who gives us the strength to pursue greatness while staying true to ourselves.

Reflection Questions

1. Who is an athlete you admire as an icon, and why?

2. How can you recognize when something—or some-one—has become an idol in your life, pulling you away from God?

— Coach Diso

20

Fruit of the Spirit: GOODNESS

"Surely your goodness and mercy will follow me all the days of my life, and I will dwell in the house of the Lord forever." — Psalm 23:6

Goodness is an active pursuit of what is right and honorable, reflecting God's character in all we do. While kindness focuses on showing love and care toward others, goodness emphasizes living in alignment with God's truth and standing up for righteousness—even when it's hard.

This verse has always been special to me because my dad loved it deeply. He believed so fully in the power of God's goodness that he actually wrote a song inspired by these words. I can still picture him singing it with conviction—his eyes closed, hands raised. That memory stuck with me. It reminded me that God's goodness isn't just a comforting idea—it's a daily promise we can hold onto.

I didn't fully understand the difference between kindness and goodness for a long time. Kindness often feels easier—it's visible in things like offering a helping hand or encouraging a teammate. But goodness sometimes demands more. It's not just about being nice. It's about doing what is right, even when it's uncomfortable or unpopular.

I remember a situation early in my coaching career when one of my players struggled academically. The kind thing might've been to offer a pass or make excuses. But the *good* thing—the right thing—was to hold him accountable. I sat him down, talked through the importance of academics, and helped create a plan for success. He didn't love it at first. Honestly, I didn't either. It was a hard conversation. But goodness isn't passive—it's active. It's about making choices that honor God's truth and help others grow. That player turned his grades around and developed the kind of responsibility that would serve him well beyond the game.

Sometimes goodness means speaking the truth when silence feels safer. It means calling out injustice, defending someone who can't speak for themselves, or standing firm in faith when culture pushes back. Jesus didn't just do good things—He *was* goodness. He healed with compassion, corrected with truth, and lived with unwavering righteousness.

As athletes, coaches, and followers of Christ, we're called to pursue this kind of goodness. It's not just about doing kind acts. It's about becoming people whose lives reflect God's truth, love, and strength—even when it costs us.

Reflection Question

What is one area in your life where you can pursue God's goodness, even if it's challenging?

— Coach Dickinson

21

The Standard

"Be perfect, therefore, as your heavenly Father is perfect" — Matthew 5:48

The life of an athlete is a lot like the journey of a Christian striving to grow in faith. Athletes set big goals and push themselves every day to get better. It's not just about the physical work—it's mental and spiritual. As a coach, I've seen countless athletes dedicate themselves to their dreams. I've also sat down with parents and players to map out plans for success. Some athletes follow the plan to the letter; others take detours, thinking they know a better way.

Sound familiar? That's how our spiritual journeys play out, too. God gives us a clear path to follow, but we often find ourselves tempted to do things our own way. Success in sports and life takes discipline, focus, and a willingness to go beyond what feels comfortable. The same is true for our walk with Christ.

When Jesus calls us to be perfect, He's not asking for flawless performance. We're human—we're going to stumble. The kind of perfection Jesus is talking about is about becoming whole — where our thoughts, words, and actions continue to reflect God's love and grace in everything we do. And here's the good news: we're not doing it to earn His love. That love is already ours — fully and completely — because of what Jesus did for us.

When we keep our eyes on Jesus, we're not driven by guilt or fear of failure. Instead, we're motivated by gratitude. We train, persevere, and aim to live lives that honor Him—not because we have to, but because we get to. And in that, there's real joy. Even when we fall short or face setbacks, those moments teach us and draw us closer to Him.

Think of your walk with Christ like training for a championship game. No athlete steps onto the field without preparation. It takes hard work, resilience, and trust in the process. You'll have challenges, but each one is an opportunity to grow stronger. Every time you choose God's way over your own, you reflect His goodness to the world.

So, what are you chasing? Is it a championship, a personal record, or something deeper? Whatever it is, remember this: when you build your life on God's foundation, you're playing for something eternal.

Reflection Questions

1. What standard in sports are you trying to live up to?

2. How did Jesus set a standard for living?

— Coach Diso

22

Fruit of the Spirit: GENTLENESS

"Let your gentleness be evident to all. The Lord is near." — Philippians 4:5

G entleness is strength under control, rooted in humility and grace—just as Christ modeled for us.

When we think of sports, gentleness might not be the first quality that comes to mind. Sports often call for intensity, aggression, and an unrelenting drive to win. But the best athletes know that true strength isn't about overpowering others—it's about channeling that intensity in a way that lifts your team and respects your opponent. Gentleness on the field looks like helping a player who's been knocked down, offering a word of encouragement to a teammate struggling, or staying calm and composed when the game doesn't go your way.

I'll be honest—gentleness wasn't a strength of mine back in the day. If it were a scale from 1 to 10, I'd probably have rated myself a solid 7... with 10 being the worst. These days, maybe on a really good day, I'd give myself a 4. Life has a way of teaching you the value of gentleness, often through people who model it in ways you'll never forget.

Raising my youngest daughter has been one of the greatest teachers of gentleness. From the moment she was born, I realized the kind of strength it takes to be patient, kind, and nurturing—even when life feels chaotic. Holding her in my arms as a baby, helping her take her first steps, and guiding her through the ups and downs of growing up required a level of gentleness I didn't know I had. Along the way, she's taught me just as much as I've taught her, and I'm grateful for how fatherhood has shaped me in this area.

Despite my struggles with gentleness, I had the privilege of growing up with a man who embodied it in a way that was anything but weak.

Coach Neff was that man. His gentleness wasn't loud or showy but quiet and powerful. I'll never forget the way he showed that gentleness when my dad passed away. It was spring break of my senior year, and I was staying at a beach condo with some FCA friends. At 4:00 a.m., the phone rang. It was Coach Neff. He told one of my buddies, "Christian needs to meet me at the hospital."

When I arrived, Coach stood at the hospital door, waiting for me. As I got closer, I sensed what had happened. My heart sank. Coach didn't say much. He just grabbed me and hugged me. When I cried out, "No, why?" he simply held me and responded, "I know, I know... then I don't know, I don't know."

At that moment, Coach Neff entered my suffering with gentleness and love. He didn't try to fix it, give me answers, or explain it away. He simply showed up, offering his strength in a way that comforted and steadied me.

Christ calls us to that kind of gentleness—a strength that chooses to walk alongside others, even in their deepest pain.

So, who comes to mind when you think of gentleness? And how can you reflect that same Christlike gentleness in your own life?

Reflection Questions

1. How can you practice Christlike gentleness in moments of frustration or conflict?

2. Who in your life models gentleness well, and what can you learn from their example?

— Coach Dickinson

23

Butterflies

"When you pass through the waters, I will be with you." — Isaiah 43:2

E very athlete knows the feeling—those pre-game jitters, the nervous energy that stirs inside before stepping onto the field. We call them "butterflies." Some players thrive on them, using that adrenaline to fuel their performance, while others let the nerves shake their confidence. I've watched countless athletes develop routines to manage those moments—repeating the same warm-up, wearing lucky gear, or going through mental checklists—all to feel ready when the whistle blows.

As a coach, I stress the importance of mental preparation. My players don't just practice physically; they take "mental reps"—visualizing success, locking in their focus, and preparing their minds for battle. That same principle applies to life. We all face moments where the weight of expectations, fear of failure, or uncertainty about the future can overwhelm us. The key is learning how to handle those feelings.

Athletes lean on their routines. But as believers, we have an even greater anchor—God's Word. When we meditate on Scripture, it resets our focus, just like Psalms 119:15 says, *"I meditate on your precepts."* Immersing our thoughts in God's Word is like mental reps—how athletes run through plays in their minds. It prepares us, strengthens us, and helps us stay ready for whatever comes our way.

This is a game-changer. When we choose to focus on God, we stop giving power to our fears. Worship replaces worry. Faith replaces doubt. We stop magnifying our problems and start magnifying Him. This doesn't mean the nerves or challenges disappear, but it does mean they don't control us.

So, whether you're gearing up for a big game or navigating life's struggles, remember this: Fix your eyes on Jesus. Trust Him in the tension. Let His Word be your playbook. When the butterflies come, don't let them shake you—let them sharpen you.

Worship Jesus—not your worries. And watch how He brings peace to every game you play and every challenge you face.

Reflection Questions

1. When did you have "butterflies," and how did you handle it?

2. What pre-game routines do you have that you could incorporate prayer into?

— Coach Diso

24

Fruit of the Spirit: SELF-CONTROL

"Everyone who competes in the games goes into strict training. They do it to get a crown that will not last, but we do it to get a crown that will last forever." — 1 Corinthians 9:25

Self-control is about personal responsibility. Unless a condition limits your ability to choose your actions, how you respond to situations is up to you. Losing your temper or flying off the handle isn't something that just "happens"—it's a choice.

Playing out scenarios ahead of time has been one of the most effective tools for learning to control my reactions. When we're surprised, we tend to show our worst side. But thinking through possible outcomes before they happen helps us stay composed, even when the unexpected arises.

Take golf, for example. If you're going to take up the sport and lack self-control, don't even bother. Golf tests your patience like nothing else. I've seen people lose their cool, break clubs, or storm off the course because of a bad shot. However, self-control is what separates players who recover from a bad hole and keep going from those who let frustration ruin their entire day.

Whether on the course, in competition, or life, self-control isn't just about keeping calm—it's about relying on Christ's strength and staying focused on what truly matters. And when you're part of a team, your lack of self-control doesn't just impact you—it impacts everyone. A single outburst, emotional meltdown, or refusal to let go of frustration can drag down your teammates, distract from the mission, and even fracture trust. Self-control protects not just your performance but the unity and focus of the whole team.

Similarly, in my weightlifting days, competition required discipline. We had three chances at meets to get our best lift of the day. That was it—no more, no less. I had to go in with a clear plan: what lifts I wanted to attempt and how I'd adjust if I missed one. Every lift came with a binary outcome. Either I succeeded and moved to a higher weight, or I failed and had to reassess and plan my next move.

Failure was part of the process, so expecting never to fail wasn't realistic. But wasting adrenaline by screaming, throwing things, or storming off after a missed lift would've only hurt my next attempt. **Adrenaline is a limited resource** in competition. You only get so many energy surges before it fades—and if you burn it all in one emotional outburst, you've got nothing left for the moments that matter most. Self-control meant conserving that energy and using it wisely.

My coaches usually guided me through those moments, reminding me to focus on what I could control and let go of what I couldn't.

Golf, weightlifting, or any other challenge in life teaches us this: self-control isn't just about avoiding outbursts—it's about managing your mind and emotions to keep moving forward. Christ modeled ultimate self-control for us, enduring trials, temptations, and even the cross with unwavering focus and strength. Just as He stayed focused on His mission, we're called to practice self-discipline in living, competing, and serving others.

Reflection Questions

1. What area of your life requires more discipline to align with God's will, whether in your relationships, habits, or emotions?

2. How can practicing self-control in your emotions impact your team, your competition, or your spiritual growth?

— Coach Dickinson

25

Change

"There is a time for everything, and a season for every activity under the heavens." — Ecclesiastes 3:1

Leadership isn't just about a title—it's about responsibility. In sports, captains don't just wear the armband or call the coin toss. They lead. They serve. They set the tone for their team. The best captains aren't just the most talented; they're the ones who show up, put in the work, and inspire others to do the same.

When I pick captains each season, I don't just look at stats. I look at character. Are they willing to shift from just being on the team to *serving* the team? Because leadership isn't about standing above—it's about bringing others up. It's about creating an environment where every teammate feels valued and respected. That's exactly what God calls us to do in our walk with Him. True leaders don't just shine when things are easy—they maintain integrity when things get tough. They stay grounded, honest, and committed to doing what's right, even when it's hard. That kind of leadership doesn't just change a team—it changes lives.

God isn't looking for people who just go through the motions. He wants hearts that are committed, not just actions that look good on the surface. That kind of faith isn't about checking boxes or following rules—it's about pursuing a real relationship with Him. When we pray, when we dive into Scripture, when we let God shape us from the inside out, *that's* when real transformation happens. And just like with great captains, that kind of faith naturally influences the people around us.

At the end of the day, true change starts from within. It's not about seeking recognition—it's about being authentic. It's about trusting God's plan and allowing Him to work through us. In leadership and in faith, the impact comes from serving with heart, staying grounded in truth, and relying on God every step of the way. When we lead like that, we don't just make a difference—we leave a legacy.

Reflection Questions

1. What qualities should captains display on and off the field?

2. How can your faith influence the way you serve others as a leader?

— Coach Diso

26

Fruit of the Spirit: FAITHFULNESS

His master replied, 'Well done, good and faithful servant! You have been faithful with a few things; I will put you in charge of many things.'" — Matthew 25:21

Faithfulness is about being dependable and consistent in your commitments, much like God's unwavering faithfulness to us. Of all the Fruits of the Spirit, faithfulness might be the one athletes identify with the most because we experience its impact firsthand.

Think about what happens when you take a few days off from training. I remember times when I got sick and couldn't work out for three or four days. That first day back was humbling. Everything felt harder—whether it was lifting weights, swinging a golf club, throwing a baseball, or hurling a javelin. I struggled to find my rhythm, and it was discouraging to see how quickly I had lost progress. Faithfulness, the habit of showing up and putting in the work consistently, isn't glamorous, but it's the difference-maker in both sports and life.

If you have the attitude of *"Put me in, Coach!"* then apply it to every situation you face. No matter how small the task, give it your absolute best. Coaches notice who puts in the effort when it doesn't seem to matter, and they notice who's just going through the motions. When it's game time, everyone wants those who took the little things seriously and committed themselves fully to the process.

The same is true in our walk with God. Faithfulness in the small things—prayer, serving others, studying Scripture—shows our dedication to Him. As we stay consistent in these areas, God entrusts us with greater opportunities to grow and serve.

Reflection Question

What small, consistent actions can you take this week to demonstrate faithfulness to your team and in your walk with God?

— Coach Dickinson

27

God Is Good

"For the Lord is good and his love endures forever; his faithfulness continues through all generations." — Psalms 100:5

As a coach, I've thrown plenty of clichés at my athletes—"Be a contender, not a pretender," or "Leave a legacy." These phrases aren't just motivational fluff; they're about building a mindset rooted in perseverance. In a world filled with expectations—whether from society, teammates, coaches, or even yourself—it's easy to feel overwhelmed. That's where faith comes in. Faith isn't just a fallback plan; it's an anchor that holds you steady through the ups and downs of competition and life.

Trusting in God's unwavering goodness isn't just about believing in something bigger—it's about *drawing strength* from it. When disappointment or uncertainty creeps in, faith turns setbacks into stepping stones. Maybe it's missing the game-winning shot or getting benched after a tough performance—those moments can either break you or build you. With the right mindset and God's strength, they become fuel to grow stronger and more focused. The passion that fuels your pursuit of greatness on the field should also drive your relationship with Christ. His love and faithfulness never waver—even when everything else feels shaky. In the pressures of competition, faith offers calm. Win or lose, there's peace in knowing God is in control. That allows athletes to play freely—not for fear of failure, but for the joy of the game and the glory of God.

There's a difference between knowing about God and truly trusting Him. Intellectual belief acknowledges His existence; heartfelt faith invites Him into every aspect of your life. When you let your faith shape your actions, it changes how you approach not just your sport but your character, leadership, and legacy. Your influence extends beyond the game—when you live out your faith, you inspire others to do the same.

So don't just chase success. Chase something deeper. Let your faith shape who you are and how you play. Because thescoreboard fades at the end of the day, but God's goodness remains. With Christ at your side, your aspirations don't just stay dreams—they become reality. The pursuit of excellence in sports mirrors the pursuit of spiritual growth. Embrace both with all your heart, knowing that true resilience comes from training your body and trusting in something greater than the game.

Reflection Questions

1. What cliché or catchphrase motivates you?

2. How can a genuine, heartfelt faith in Jesus help you excel?

— Coach Diso

28

Who Rules the Earth?

"We know that we are children of God, and that the whole world is under the control of the evil one." — 1 John 5:19

"I have told you these things, so that in me you may have peace. In this world you will have trouble. But take heart! I have overcome the world." — John 16:33

The Bible refers to Satan as the "prince of this world." While this might feel unsettling, it's a reminder that our world is deeply flawed and marred by sin. When Jesus came to earth, many expected Him to reign as a physical king, using power and authority to overthrow oppressors. Even His disciples misunderstood His mission. Jesus humorously nicknamed James and John the "Sons of Thunder"—perhaps because they, too, anticipated a Messiah who would rule with lightning and strike down all who opposed Him.

As athletes, we often fall into a similar mindset. We believe victory is all about physical dominance—outmuscling, outworking, and overpowering the competition. But Jesus showed us a different kind of leadership and victory. His mission wasn't about conquering through force but about transforming hearts to build an eternal Kingdom.

I've experienced this struggle personally. I often had my eyes on the wrong prize—a title, a record, money, or recognition. While I sometimes achieved these goals, they never quite satisfied me like I thought they would. When my aim was solely for earthly accolades, that was the most I could achieve. But when I shifted my focus to honoring God and serving His purpose, I found true fulfillment—regardless of the outcome.

In sports, we face challenges that can feel like battles. The world often rewards selfishness, pride, and shortcuts. But as followers of Christ, we're called to live differently. We're called to compete with integrity, lead with humility, and trust God's bigger plan—just as Jesus did.

Real victory is found in honoring God, not in worldly wins. Satan's rule on earth is limited, and the eternal Kingdom of God is where our focus should lie.

Reflection Question

How can you honor God as an athlete today, knowing that true victory comes from serving His eternal Kingdom rather than chasing worldly recognition? Can you be victorious in both kingdoms? Absolutely.

— Coach Dickinson

29

Storms of Purpose

"He stilled the storm to a whisper." — Psalms 107:29

E very athlete knows the feeling—a new season, team, and challenges. It's like stepping onto the field or court for the first time all over again. The uncertainty, the nerves, the pressure to prove yourself can feel like a storm rolling in, unpredictable and overwhelming.

Starting over can be daunting, but it also presents invaluable growth opportunities. Each new season brings its own unique hurdles—learning different strategies, adjusting to unfamiliar coaching styles, and finding your place within a new team dynamic. It's easy to feel anxious, even lost at times, wondering if you'll measure up or if you'll belong.

But here's the thing about storms—they have a purpose. They shake things up, clear the path, and make way for something greater. Maybe you're stepping into a leadership role for the first time or learning how to work alongside teammates with different styles and personalities. Growth isn't always comfortable, but it's necessary.

This is where faith comes in. Trusting in God through uncertain times gives us strength to push forward. Instead of fearing the unknown, we can recognize that every new season is part of a bigger plan. God has already paved the way—you just have to step forward in faith.

Remember, God doesn't call you to comfort; He calls you to purpose. Every setback, adjustment, and unfamiliar challenge shapes you into the athlete, leader, and person He designed you to be. When the storms roll in, don't panic. Trust. Lean in. Know that God is with you and will calm the chaos in His perfect time.

So, as you enter new seasons—whether in sports or life—don't let fear hold you back. Embrace the challenge, trust the process, and know that even in uncertainty, you are right where you should be.

Reflection Questions

1. What are the biggest challenges when starting over?

2. How can stepping into something new stretch your faith?

— Coach Diso

30

Persevering Through Pain

"Consider it pure joy...when you face trials of many kinds, because you know the testing of your faith produces perseverance." — James 1:2-4

P ain is something every athlete faces—whether it's physical, mental, or emotional. Maybe it's the burn in your legs during conditioning drills, the sting of a heartbreaking loss, or the long road to recovery after an injury. Pain in the moment never feels good. But it often leads to something greater. That's true in athletics, and it's true in our walk with Christ.

James isn't telling us to enjoy pain—he's telling us to see its purpose. Trials of any kind become opportunities to grow in perseverance. When our faith is tested, it produces endurance that transforms us.

When I suffered an injury that paused my golf career, it wasn't just the physical setback that hit me. I missed the camaraderie of the mini-tour—being with teammates, trading stories, and living life together. Instead, I was alone with my thoughts and frustrations.

That season forced me to dig deeper—not just to heal my body but to strengthen my spirit.

I thought about Jesus in the Garden of Gethsemane. He knew suffering was coming, and even then, He asked His disciples to stay and pray with Him. That moment shows us something powerful: even Jesus didn't want to suffer alone. And He doesn't ask us to, either.

As athletes, we get that. When a teammate is injured, we rally around them. When someone is hurting, we show up. Whether it's taping an ankle, saying a prayer, or just sitting in silence, those small acts echo what Christ modeled—entering into someone else's pain.

So when James says to "consider it joy," it's not about pretending everything is fine. It's about knowing that God uses our trials—on and off the field—to refine us. He shapes us through suffering, and He often does it through the people He's placed beside us.

If you're going through something hard, don't isolate. Invite others in. And if someone around you is hurting, don't walk past their pain. Step into it. That's what teammates do. That's what Jesus did.

Reflection Questions

1. How can perseverance in your faith shape how you face challenges in other areas?

2. Who in your life is going through a trial, and how can you step into their suffering to support them?

— Coach Dickinson

31

God's Plan

"For I know the plans I have for you," declares the Lord, "plans to prosper you and not to harm you, plans to give you hope and a future." — Jeremiah 29:11

Life has a way of knocking us down. Disappointments, setbacks, and losses can make us question whether a bigger plan is in place. Over the years, I've coached athletes who've been through more than most people realize—battles that don't just test their strength on the field but their faith in what's ahead. The truth is God's plan doesn't always unfold the way we expect, but it's always working for our good.

Take Andy. When he started high school, he was carrying the weight of losing his mom just a year before. That grief showed up as anger and rebellion, and it cost him. His coaches didn't see past the surface, and their discouragement only reinforced his belief that he'd never be enough. Eventually, he left that school mid-year.

The next fall, Andy showed up on my doorstep. He was still carrying the same pain, but something was different—he was searching. We had honest, faith-driven conversations about surrendering control to God. We discussed what it means to trust that His plan is bigger than our disappointments. Little by little, Andy started making a choice: to let go of the anger that was holding him back and lean into the purpose God had for him.

Over the next three years, I watched him transform—not just as an athlete but as a person. He realized that real strength isn't just about physical ability; it's about having the faith to release what's weighing you down. By shifting his focus from his pain to his purpose, he became a Division 1 athlete and earned a full scholarship to college.

Andy's story is proof that when we surrender to God's plan, we step into something greater than we ever imagined. Your past doesn't define you, and your setbacks aren't the end of the story. Every struggle can be a step closer to what God has in store—if you're willing to trust Him.

Reflection Questions

1. What in your past are you still holding on to?

2. How could letting go of disappointment help you move forward toward your goals?

— **Coach Diso**

32

If I Could Only Teach You Three Things

To become a Christian and grow in faith, you must first be **grounded in truth**—understanding who God is and what He has revealed. Next, how we **invest our time** determines who we become because our daily choices shape our walk with Christ. Finally, true transformation is rooted in fully **grasping the unconditional love** of our Heavenly Father, which gives us security, identity, and purpose.

If you were to take only three devotions from this book to heart, let them be these:

1. **Big T Truth** *(Chapter 33)* — The foundation of faith begins with knowing God and standing firm in His Word. Without truth, everything else crumbles.

2. **Time: Your Greatest Superpower** *(Chapter 34)* — How we spend our time determines our growth, closeness to Christ, and readiness to be used by Him.

3. **Loved** *(Chapter 35)* — Understanding God's deep, unwavering love changes everything. It defines who we are and how we live.

Maybe you already know these truths and have them firmly rooted in your heart—that's a wonderful thing. But sometimes, hearing them framed in a new way helps organize our thoughts and equips us to share our faith with others. Even if nothing else sticks, this three-part framework can help you recognize where someone is in their journey:

- Are they searching for truth?

- Are they struggling to invest their time wisely?

- Are they wrestling with whether they are truly loved?

When we understand where a person stands, we know better how to pray for them, support them, and meet them where they are.

A verse that ties all three pillars together is John 17:17-19, where Jesus prays for His disciples:

"Sanctify them by the truth; Your word is truth. As You sent Me into the world, I also have sent them into the world. I sanctify Myself for them, so that they also may be sanctified by the truth." (CSB)

Jesus Himself points to truth, purpose, and transformation through love. These aren't just principles for spiritual growth—they are foundations for excellence in every area of life, including athletics.

The best athletes aren't just skilled—they're grounded in truth about who they are, disciplined with their time, and fueled by a deep sense of purpose. When you build your life on these three foundations spiritually, everything else—including how you train, compete, and lead—will be shaped by Christ.

Take these three truths seriously. Let them drive your growth, fuel your excellence, and become part of the testimony you live out every single day.

— Coach Dickinson

33

1/3 Big T Truth

"Therefore everyone who hears these words of mine and puts them into practice is like a wise man who built his house on the rock. The rain came down, the streams rose, and the winds blew and beat against that house; yet it did not fall, because it had its foundation on the rock." — Matthew 7:24-25 (NIV)

A strong foundation is everything. Ask any athlete—without proper footing, success is nearly impossible. A quarterback must plant their feet before throwing a deep pass. A batter's stance determines the power of their swing. A runner needs solid ground to explode off the starting line. Without stability, even the most skilled athlete will stumble.

The same is true in life. But here's the problem—our world is playing on shifting sand. Society tells us "truth" is whatever you want it to be. "Live your truth," they say, as if the truth is flexible, personal, and ever-changing. But truth is not something we create—truth is something we discover. And God reveals **The Truth** to us through His Word.

For 2,000 years, skeptics have tried to discredit, distort, and destroy the Bible. Yet despite every attack, Scripture has stood the test of time. History, archaeology, fulfilled prophecy, and personal transformation all confirm its reliability. If the Bible was true then and is true now, it will be true forever.

The world will tell you that deception is just a "strategy," that lying is acceptable if it serves your agenda, and that twisting words to fit your desires is the new definition of "truth." But Jesus didn't say, "I am a truth." He said, **"I am the way, the truth, and the life"** (John 14:6).

Truth isn't an idea. It's not an opinion. It's a person.

Truth has a name—and His name is Jesus.

When you build your life on Jesus, you're not just standing on a set of beliefs but on God's living, unshakable foundation. His words, life, and resurrection prove that truth doesn't change with the times, trends, or feelings. It endures forever.

So here's the question: What are you standing on? You'll fall every time if your foundation is built on cultural opinions, feelings, or personal interpretations of truth. But if you plant your feet firmly on God's Word—a truth that never changes—you'll stand strong, no matter what comes your way.

Reflection Question

Are you building your life on the unchanging truth of God's Word or on the shifting opinions of the world? What steps can you take to stay grounded in truth?

— Coach Dickinson

34

2/3 Time: Your Greatest Superpower

"There is a time for everything, and a season for every activity under the heavens." — Ecclesiastes 3:1

Time is fascinating. We live within its boundaries—24 hours in a day, seven days in a week, 365.25 days in a year, 10 years in a decade, and 10 decades in a century. Those are the limits of most human lives. But God? He exists outside of time—eternal, without beginning or end.

Here on earth, though, time is our greatest asset. Why? Because how we spend it determines our future—both in the relationships we build now and in our eternity to come. We only have so much time here, but how we use it will echo forever.

I know firsthand how investing time pays off. Injuries aside, I found success in weightlifting and golf—two sports that demand relentless dedication. When I was immersed in golf, I wasn't just playing; I was living the game. I studied swings, practiced every spare minute, and even slept with my putter beside my bed, visualizing strokes before drifting off. Perfect practice—careful, intentional practice—built muscle memory that I could trust under pressure.

But it wasn't just about time spent but about **how** that time was spent. Poor habits practiced over and over became permanent just as easily as good ones. If my grip was wrong or my stance was off, and I kept repeating it, my body locked in those mistakes. Perfect practice doesn't just make perfect—it makes **permanent**. Excellence becomes second nature only when excellence is deliberately and consistently practiced.

The same principle applies to our Christian walk. We strengthen our spiritual instincts every day. We invest in prayer, Scripture, obedience, and living like Christ. Righteousness becomes our reflex because we've trained ourselves to walk in the Spirit.

Ephesians 5:15–16 puts it plainly: **"Be very careful, then, how you live—not as unwise but as wise, making the most of every opportunity, because the days are evil."** (NIV)

If that was true when Paul wrote it, how much more urgent is it today?

Technology has made time management harder than ever. Social media, YouTube, video games, and endless notifications are designed to capture and keep your attention. Five minutes turns into fifty without even realizing it. Technology isn't evil, but without discipline, it can quietly rob you of your most valuable resource: time.

God modeled intentional time from the beginning. He walked with Adam and Eve. He invested in Moses, David, and the prophets. Jesus, too, managed His time purposefully—investing deeply in a few before ministering to the many. He knew that strong relationships weren't built accidentally. They required consistent, focused time.

It's the same with us. Coaches build champions by investing hours upon hours in their players. Parents shape futures by being present day after day. Strong faith, strong families, and strong futures all share one thing in common: **time intentionally spent**.

Looking back, I wish I had evaluated my time more carefully. I would have made better decisions. And that's why I'm urging you—don't just drift through your days. Time is passing, whether you steward it or not.

The world will throw distraction after distraction your way—it's a battle for your attention. But God has given you a choice. You can take control of your time and invest it in what matters most or let it slip through your fingers.

If you can master your time, you will master one of the greatest keys to living a life that honors God.

Reflection Question

Are you making the most of the time God has given you? Are today's choices drawing you closer to Him—or are they slipping away unnoticed?

— Coach Dickinson

My Dad

My dad's job
publish magazine

My favorite thing
to do with my dad
help cook

My dad's superpower
problem solving

I love Dad more than
an elephant

My dad always laughs when
I tell him a joke

I love my dad because
he plays with me
& cooks good
food.

**MY TIME REPORT
CARD FROM DARCY
(ALMOST 6)**

TIME

TIME

TIME

TIME

TIME

35

3/3 Loved

"We love because He first loved us." — 1 John 4:19

Love is the foundation of our faith. Before we ever sought God, He loved us. Before we did anything to deserve it—before we even existed—His love was already there. Many people struggle to believe this. We live in a world where love is often conditional, based on performance, behavior, or meeting expectations. But God's love is different. It is constant, unchanging, and freely given.

For some, accepting the love of our Heavenly Father feels natural. But for others, it can feel distant—even impossible. How our earthly fathers or authority figures treated us often shapes how we see God. If you've experienced neglect, verbal or physical abuse, broken trust, or any kind of pain at the hands of someone who was supposed to care for you, you might feel an invisible barrier between you and God. You may wonder, *How could a Father truly love me unconditionally?*

But here is the truth: God is not a reflection of your earthly father; He is the perfection of fatherhood. He is steady where others have wavered, safe where others have harmed, and present where others have abandoned.

Healing from past wounds is not about forgetting—it's about understanding the damage that has been done and learning how to move forward. If your past experiences have made it challenging to grasp God's love, know this: you don't have to walk that journey alone. Talking to a trusted mentor, pastor, or Christian counselor can be vital to healing. God's love doesn't erase your past, but it can redeem it—by walking with you through the pain and leading you toward healing, wholeness, and hope. Taking that first step might mean opening up to someone you trust and allowing them to walk alongside you as you process your story. You are not alone in this journey.

As an athlete, you may know the pressure to perform—to earn a coach's approval, a starting spot, or the cheers of a crowd. Maybe you felt valued when you played well and overlooked when you didn't. Maybe the compliments only came after a win, while the mistakes were magnified after a loss. Over time, it's easy to believe that love, acceptance, and identity are things you must earn—and that failure diminishes your worth.

Sadly, many carry this mindset into their relationship with God. We start thinking we must "perform" spiritually—pray enough, serve enough, behave perfectly—to keep His love. We imagine God as a coach on the sideline, approving only when we succeed.

But the truth is, God's love is **not based on our performance**. It's based on His character. He doesn't love you more when you "win" or less when you "lose." His love isn't something you achieve—it's something you **receive**.

The moment you grasp the depth of God's love, everything changes. You stop striving for approval and start living in the security of His grace. You stop fearing failure because you realize you are already fully known and fully loved. And you find the freedom to love others better—because you're no longer trying to earn what has already been given.

If this devotion resonates with you and you want to explore this truth more deeply, I encourage you to read *Loved* by my good friend Nick Vasiliades. His book beautifully unpacks the life-changing reality of God's unconditional love.

Reflection Questions

Do you truly believe that God loves you unconditionally?

How has your experience with earthly love—whether good or painful—shaped your view of God's love?

What steps can you take to heal from past wounds and fully embrace His perfect love?

— Coach Dickinson

36

Be Deliberate

"Restore to me the joy of your salvation and grant me a willing spirit, to sustain me."—Psalm 51:12

Let's get one thing straight—when I first started playing football, I had no clue what I was doing. I grew up on baseball and basketball, so stepping onto the football field felt like stepping onto another planet. The speed, physicality, and intensity were all brand new. And let's be real: self-doubt is a beast. I questioned myself constantly. *Am I good enough? Do I belong here?*

That's where Coach Dickinson came in. He wasn't just a coach; he was a mentor, a guide, and one of the most consistent voices in my life. His door was always open, whether I needed to talk about playing time or just vent about my day. He made time. He listened. And his advice? It wasn't just about football—it was about life.

But the biggest lesson he taught me? *Be deliberate.*

Faith isn't just a box to check. It's not about showing up to church, saying a quick prayer before bed, or tossing a "Thanks, God" when things go our way. It's about intentionally seeking Jesus—every day, in every moment. Prayer isn't just words; it's connection. Our faith isn't just a thing we *have*—it's a relationship we *build*.

Coach Dickinson lived that out. He reminded me that honoring God isn't just something we *do*—it's who we *are*. It's in the way we think, the way we act, the way we treat people. When we're deliberate about chasing after Christ, it changes us. And when it changes us, it impacts everyone around us—our family, teammates, and community.

Looking back, I see now that Coach Dickinson wasn't just coaching us on the field. He was coaching us for life. And the lesson is simple but powerful: *Be deliberate. Seek Jesus with intention. Honor Him in everything.*

Because in the end, it's not just about what we accomplish—it's about who we become.

Reflection Questions

1. Who is one person you go to when you need advice?

2. Why is it important to be intentional in your relationship with Jesus?

— Coach Diso

37

The Power of Preparation

"Everyone who competes in the games goes into strict training." – 1 Corinthians 9:25

An athlete understands that success isn't accidental—it's intentional. They wake up early for workouts, stay up late studying film, follow strict nutrition plans, and sacrifice time with friends to train. Every sprint, every rep, every disciplined choice is done with a future goal in mind. They don't just train for the sake of training; they train with the expectation that their preparation will be tested in competition one day.

The same is true for our spiritual lives. As followers of Christ, we are called to a life of discipline—not just for some distant future, but for today. Unlike an athlete who can point to a specific date for their championship game, we don't know when we'll face a spiritual battle, a trial, or even the moment when our faith will be tested. That's why we must prepare daily—through prayer, scripture, and intentional spiritual discipline.

Paul reminds us in **1 Timothy 4:8**, *"For physical training is of some value, but godliness has value for all things, holding promise for both* *the present life and the life to come."* Just as athletes condition their bodies, Christians must train their hearts and minds for spiritual endurance. The work we put in today—prayer, studying God's Word, resisting temptation—prepares us for the challenges ahead.

For an athlete, this might mean waking up early to pray before heading to the weight room, listening to worship music while stretching, staying in the Christian community despite a packed schedule, or making time to study God's Word between classes and practices. It's about training the heart and soul with the same dedication as training the body.

Jesus Himself modeled this discipline. **Mark 1:35** says, *"Very early in the morning, while it was still dark, Jesus got up, left the house, and went off to a solitary place, where he prayed."* If the Son of God saw the need to prepare through prayer, how much more should we?

The reality is this: the time to prepare isn't when the game is on the line—it's long before you step onto the field. Spiritually, the same principle applies. It may be too late if you wait until the pressure is on to start strengthening your faith. **Ephesians 6:13** urges us, *"Therefore put on the full armor of God, so that when the day of evil comes, you may be able to stand your ground, and after you have done everything, to stand."*

The discipline of preparation is what separates the good from the great—not just in sports, but in faith. Will you be ready when the moment comes?

Reflection Questions

- What does your spiritual "training" look like in your daily routine?

- How can discipline in your athletic life translate to your faith walk?

- In what areas do you need to be more intentional about your spiritual preparation?

— Coach Dickinson

38

Godly Examples

"Whoever pursues righteousness and love finds life, prosperity, and honor." — Proverbs 21:21

E very team has different types of athletes. You've got the work-horses who grind every day, the naturals who make it look easy, the hype guys who bring the energy, and the ones just trying to be part of something bigger than themselves. Each one plays a role. Each one matters.

But let's be real—competition can bring out the best *and* the worst in us. It can push us to be great but also stir up jealousy, pride, and division. When one teammate gets all the glory, others might feel overlooked. And when winning becomes more important than the people around us, we lose sight of what really matters.

That's why being a Godly example isn't just about working hard or being the best player—it's about lifting others up. It's about showing respect, encouragement, and love, no matter your role on the team. Jesus didn't play favorites. He valued *everyone*. And if we're serious about following Him, we've got to do the same.

So how do we do that? We celebrate each other's wins. We push each other to be better. We remind our teammates that their worth isn't just in their stats but in who they are in Christ. A team that supports each other—that's a team that thrives. And when we pursue righteousness and love, just like Proverbs 21:21 says, we find something greater than success. We find purpose.

Reflection Questions

1. What type of athlete would you consider yourself?

2. How is your faith impacting your teammates?

— Coach Diso

39

Humility Wins

"Do nothing out of selfish ambition or vain conceit. Rather, in humility value others above yourselves." — Philippians 2:3

Humility and winning—it feels like an oxymoron, doesn't it? Kind of like "jumbo shrimp" or "deafening silence." When we win, we want to stand tall, soak in the moment, and feel that rush of pride. But does humility have a place on the winner's podium? Can we be both proud of our success and humble in our hearts? The answer is yes—but it takes intentional effort.

Humility doesn't mean shrinking or pretending you're less capable than you are. It means recognizing that your success isn't yours alone. It's built on the shoulders of coaches, teammates, and opponents who push you to improve. Most importantly, it's built on the shoulders of the Creator, who gave each of us the measure of talent we need to develop.

True leaders understand this. They celebrate victories without letting their egos get in the way and use their platform to lift others up. I remember standing next to Coach Diso as a player every time he was interviewed after a game. He always attributed his success to the offensive line, receivers, and his fellow coaches. He never soaked in the glory for himself. Instead, he turned around and credited the people around him who helped make the victory possible.

That act of humility didn't make him any less of a hero—it made him more of one. The team respected him even more because he valued others above himself. It reminded me of the verse in Philippians and its connection to another passage: "Humble yourselves in the sight of the Lord, and He will lift you up." At first, it feels like an oxymoron—humbling yourself leads to being lifted up? But that's precisely how God works. When we put Him and others first and keep ourselves grounded, He's the one who exalts us at the right time.

Reflecting on this, I realized the two people who most clearly modeled humility for me were Coach Neff and Diso—one as a coach and the other as a player. Everyone has an ego, but I've never seen theirs in the 30 years I've known them. And maybe that's the point of humility. True humility isn't just an act—it's an unseen quality, something deeply woven into your character that speaks louder than words.

Winning with humility means appreciating the moment while remembering the bigger picture. It's not about downplaying the victory; it's about keeping your ego in check and staying grounded. It's about saying, "I'm proud of what we've done together," and recognizing the God-given gifts that made it all possible.

Reflection Questions

1. How can humility strengthen your relationships with teammates, coaches, and others?

2. In what areas of your life—on and off the field—do you
   need to practice humility?

— Coach Dickinson

40

Renew

"Do not conform to the pattern of this world, but be transformed by the renewing of your mind." — Romans 12:2

K evin showed up as a freshman, wide-eyed and eager to get better. He dove into the sport headfirst, spending hours watching highlight reels and studying every move of the pros, convinced that if he just mimicked their mechanics, he'd be elite in no time. It's a great mindset—to be hungry to learn—but it comes with a trap.

See, in the digital age, we have instant access to greatness. One swipe, one click, and we're staring at the best of the best—accomplishments, rankings, highlight plays. And if we're not careful, that inspiration can turn into pressure. Instead of fueling us, it drains us. Instead of pushing us forward, it makes us feel like we'll never measure up. I saw that struggle in Kevin. The fire to improve was there, but so was the frustration. He wanted to be great overnight.

That's why renewal is so important. To renew means to breathe life back into something—to refresh, restore, and refocus. And the best way to do that? Through Christ. When we let Him shape our thoughts, we stop letting the world's measuring sticks define us. Instead of getting lost in comparisons, we start running our own race, embracing the process.

But renewal isn't automatic. It's intentional. You don't just *hope* to get stronger—you train. You don't just *wish* to get faster—you work. The same goes for faith. If we want to be transformed, we must be in His Word, in His presence, letting Him renew us daily.

Kevin eventually figured that out. He stopped worrying about how he stacked up against others and started focusing on steady improvement. And you know what? He got better—stronger, smarter, more confident. Not because he copied someone else perfectly but because he learned to trust his own growth.

In a world obsessed with instant success, be the one who embraces the grind. True growth takes time. Stay rooted in Christ, and let Him shape your path—not the rankings, highlights, or noise. That's real renewal.

Reflection Questions

1. Who's an athlete you try to emulate? What do you admire about them?

2. How does having a heart and mind for God help you grow—not just in sports, but in life?

—Coach Diso

41

Stay in Position

"Be still before the Lord and wait patiently for him." — Psalm 37:7

At a time in my life, I got caught up in the mindset of chasing the "next big thing." It felt contagious, especially in a culture—and on social media—that constantly pushes what's new, trending, and next. I bought into it because some people around me always talked about how they'd do things better if they were in a different position or situation. The more I scrolled, the more it seemed everyone else was already there—living the life I wanted.

Over time, I began to see a pattern. Those people were never satisfied; they weren't excelling at their jobs, and most of them never achieved the goals they were chasing. That realization became a turning point for me. I started to embrace the phrase *Carpe Diem*—seize the day—because today is all we are promised.

Psalm 37:7 reminds us to "be still before the Lord and wait patiently for him." That verse is a powerful reminder to trust God's timing. When we focus on the moment He has given us, we honor Him and grow stronger and more prepared for the future. God provides for our needs daily—shelter, food, and clothing. Yesterday is gone, and tomorrow isn't guaranteed. Today is His gift to us, and He calls us to give it our all.

Jesus also teaches in **Luke 16:10**, *"Whoever can be trusted with very little can also be trusted with much."* If we neglect what is in front of us, always chasing the next big thing, we miss the chance to grow and steward what God has already placed in our hands. When we are faithful in the small stuff—whether working hard in practice, showing up for teammates, or being diligent in our responsibilities—God sees that, and it prepares us for greater things in His perfect timing.

As athletes, we can embrace this mindset by showing up fully in practice and games, giving everything we have to the moment. As the saying goes, *"Leave it all on the field."* That's how we should approach every day of our lives. When someone asks, *"How was your day?"* let your answer be, *"I gave it my all—that's all I can do, and God will do the rest."*

Reflection Questions

1. How can patience benefit your spiritual life?

2. Are you trusting God's timing?

— Coach Dickinson

42

Faith or Fear

**"There is no fear in love. But perfect love drives out fear, because fear has to do with punishment. The one who fears is not made in perfect love" —
1 John 4:18**

F ear often lurks in the shadows in playing and coaching sports, ready to pounce at the most critical moments. As athletes and coaches, we experience this common anxiety—whether standing at the free throw line, gripping a bat in a batter's box, during a timeout when the game is on the line, or preparing to tee off. It's a universal truth that athletes must confront their fears, grappling with self-doubt and the weight of expectations.

Mike, one of my former athletes, symbolized this struggle. Despite his unwavering work ethic and an intense desire to achieve greatness, he was haunted by the fear of failure. I saw in him the potential that he and others often overlooked, believing wholeheartedly that he could rise to the occasion. Mike learned to confront and ultimately transcend his fears through our journey together. His hard work culminated when he led his team to their first-ever championship title, securing his legacy in the school's Hall of Fame.

This triumph was a testament to his athletic ability and a powerful reflection of how he harnessed his faith to drive out fear. Faith and fear are often at odds. We cannot truly know God, love Him, or obey His will without leaning into faith.

Fear is the greatest adversary to this faith, clouding our vision and complicating our journeys. Living in fear is to deny the existence of a higher power, believing that we alone must navigate life's uncertainties. It attempts to control what is often uncontrollable, diminishing our capacity for trust. However, God's love acts as a blanket for our fears. Time and again, scripture reminds us to "Fear Not."

This divine reassurance encourages us to relinquish control over our lives and circumstances. Through faith—a gift from God—we find peace and strength. When we submit our fears and uncertainties to Jesus, our faith flourishes, and we become capable of remarkable feats. Embracing faith means letting go of the need for control and trusting in God's plan. It requires courage to step into the unknown, but the rewards for those who seek Him are profound. By casting our fears aside and placing our lives in His hands, we open ourselves to new possibilities and experiences, allowing God to renew our spirits and guide our paths. As we reflect on our journeys as athletes and leaders, remember that fear does not define us. Instead, our faith shapes our destinies and empowers us to achieve greatness against all odds. Trust in God, submit your fears, and watch as He transforms your life in ways you never thought possible.

Reflection Questions

1. What specific moment in your sport did fear take control?

2. How can our faith in God drive our fear in moments of stress?

—Coach Diso

43

Playing for an Audience of One

"Whatever you do, work at it with all your heart, as working for the Lord, not for human masters."
— Colossians 3:23

As athletes, it's easy to get caught up in playing for the crowd's cheers, the approval of coaches, or the recognition of teammates. We work hard for the applause, the trophy, or the accolades that come with success. But as followers of Christ, we are called to a higher purpose—to play for an audience of One.

I'll never forget the moment I made a 47-yard field goal. For 5.7 seconds, I was on top of the world. The crowd roared, my teammates celebrated, and I soaked in that fleeting moment of glory. You may remember this story from the chapter on peace—and it's worth repeating. Because what stuck with me wasn't the applause—it was what happened before the kick. I could feel the pressure mounting as I stood there, lining up the attempt. The crowd's noise was deafening, and the moment's weight pressed hard on my shoulders.

Right then, I prayed a simple prayer: I asked God to help me drown out all the noise and focus solely on the kick at hand. That prayer gave me a peace I can't fully explain. It was as if the entire crowd faded away, and it was just me, the ball, and God. When I made the kick, the crowd's roar was glorious—but temporary. What stayed with me, even to this day, was the intimate encounter I had with the Lord at that moment.

This experience taught me an important lesson. The cheers and applause we chase as athletes feel great, but they don't last. However, when we focus on honoring God with our efforts, we gain something far greater—His presence, peace, and affirmation. Colossians 3:23 reminds us that whatever we do—on the field, in the classroom, or at work—we ultimately work for the Lord. When we play for Him, the pressure to perform fades. Whether we succeed or fail, we can rest in the unshakable truth that our identity is anchored in Christ, not in the fleeting approval of others.

So, the next time you step onto the field or face a challenge, ask yourself: Who am I playing for? Let your answer be clear: you're playing for an audience of One.

Reflection Questions

1. Whose approval are you seeking most in your life?

2. How can shifting your focus to God bring you peace and purpose?

— Coach Dickinson

44

Eyes

"Fix our eyes on Jesus, the author and perfecter of our faith." — Hebrews 12:2

P ressure is part of the game. As athletes, we face expectations from coaches, teammates, parents, and even ourselves. It's easy to let the fear of failure creep in—to dwell on past mistakes, overthink the moment, and psych ourselves out before we even get started. And when that happens, it doesn't just affect us individually; it impacts the whole team.

I remember a game where my coach called me in as a pinch hitter with the score tied. I'd put in the work—I spent hours in the cages, preparing for moments like this. But right before I stepped up to the plate, my coach threw me a curveball: "Hit left-handed."

I had been training as a switch hitter but wasn't confident in it yet. The doubts hit hard. *What if I strike out? What if I let the team down?* I walked up to the plate, already defeated in my mind. I managed to make contact—grounding out on a fielder's choice that brought in a run—but looking back, I realize my biggest opponent wasn't the pitcher. It was my own fear.

When we let anxiety and self-doubt take over, we lose sight of the bigger picture. That's why Hebrews 12:2 tells us to fix our eyes on Jesus. Everything changes when we shift our focus from the pressure and expectations to Him. Putting *on our 'Jesus Eyes'* means seeing beyond the moment—beyond the fear and circumstances—and locking in on the One who never wavers.

Jesus gives us peace that doesn't depend on the scoreboard. When we fix our eyes on Him, we play confidently, knowing that our worth isn't in our performance but His love. The ultimate prize isn't a championship—it's the unwavering joy, purpose, and peace we find in Christ. If I ever get the opportunity to step up to the plate again, I know that keeping my eyes on Jesus will silence every doubt.

Reflection Questions

1. Think of a time when negative thoughts affected your performance. What happened?

2. How would fixing your eyes on Jesus have changed that moment?

— **Coach Diso**

45

It All Goes Back in the Box

"For what does it profit a man to gain the whole world and forfeit his soul?" — Mark 8:36

When I was a kid, my grandmother, Nana, loved playing Scrabble with me. She beat me every time until I was about 16. I remember the first time I finally won a game fair and square. She smiled at me and said, "In the end, it all goes back in the box."

At the time, I didn't think much about what she meant. I chalked it up to something a loser says, too caught up in my moment of victory to care. I celebrated with a little victory dance, never realizing there was a lesson buried in her words.

My dad, however, often gave me a different kind of reminder. When I was about to make a decision—especially one rooted in pride or selfishness—he would simply quote this verse: *"For what does it profit a man to gain the whole world and forfeit his soul?"* He wouldn't explain or elaborate; he didn't need to. The verse stood on its own, challenging me to think about the bigger picture and the impact of my actions.

Years later, while I was an assistant coach, those words came back to me. One Friday night, our team faced a rival coached by someone who had once been my high school coach. By halftime, the score was 38-0—not in our favor. I stood on the sideline, young and learning, as our head coach tried to motivate the players with a halftime speech about resilience and pride.

By the fourth quarter, it was 63-0, and I witnessed something I'd never seen before: my team's hope shattered. I didn't have the authority to change the situation, but I had a front-row seat to an important lesson about sportsmanship. The opposing coach had already won, yet he chose to press on with his starters, missing a powerful opportunity to model grace.

What stuck with me most is that I remember the score, but most people don't. They remember how a former coach made them feel that night. The sting of humiliation overshadowed any pride or joy in the victory. It reminded me that leadership is measured less by success and more by humility—something Jesus modeled perfectly. Though He had all authority, He chose the path of service, not domination. In sports and life, that kind of humility leaves a mark that outlasts any scoreboard.

My grandmother's words ring true: "It all goes back in the box." The victories, the trophies, and the accolades all fade away with time. But the feelings you leave with others—those stay. In the end, how you made someone feel stays, but everything else "goes back in the box."

Reflection Question

How can you ensure your victories, whether in sports or life, are marked by humility and kindness rather than pride?

— Coach Dickinson

46

Up to God

"In their hearts humans plan their course, but the Lord establishes their steps." — Proverbs 16:9

Faith, prayer, and trusting God—whether in victory or defeat—are things every athlete wrestles with. It's natural to hope for certain outcomes, to work hard, and to expect success. But what happens when the results don't go our way? When the prayers for a win, a personal record, or a big moment on the field don't pan out?

I remember a pregame Bible study in which one of my athletes prayed specifically for personal stats. Now, I get it—athletes want to perform well. But something about that moment stuck with me. It highlighted how easy it is to fall into the trap of seeing prayer as a way to get what we want rather than a way to align ourselves with God.

Here's the reality: Faith isn't about asking for favorable results. It's about trusting God no matter what. Losses can teach us just as much—if not more—than victories. When things don't go as planned, we have a choice: get frustrated or trust that God's got something bigger in the works.

This is where gratitude comes in. When we shift our focus from *'Why didn't this happen for me?'* to *'What is God teaching me through this?'* our entire perspective changes. That's how we grow. That's how we develop the kind of faith that isn't shaken by a bad game or a tough break.

That's why renewing our minds with God's truth is critical—just like Romans 12:12 encourages us: *"Be joyful in hope, patient in affliction, faithful in prayer."* The world—and even our thoughts—will try to convince us we're only as good as our last performance. But when we stay rooted in Scripture, we remember who we are in Christ: loved, valued, and called for a greater purpose.

Reflection Question

How can you align your prayers with God's will for you as an athlete?

— Coach Diso

47

God is Everywhere

"For in him all things were created: things in heaven and on earth, visible and invisible, whether thrones or powers or rulers or authorities; all things have been created through him and for him." — Colossians 1:16 (NIV)

"The heavens declare the glory of God; the skies proclaim the work of his hands." — Psalm 19:1 (NIV)

Have you ever stopped to see God's fingerprints in your daily life? In TobyMac's song *"Everything,"* he sings, *"I see You in everything, all day."* These lyrics remind us that God is not distant but present in every corner of our world. Whether it's the beauty of nature, the smile of a friend, or even the grind of a hard workout, God's handiwork is everywhere if we take the time to notice.

As athletes, we might feel like God's presence is limited to Sunday mornings or prayer time. But the truth is, He's right there in the early-morning practices, in the sweat and determination, and in the victories and defeats. He's in the discipline it takes to train, and the camaraderie shared with teammates. When we open our hearts and look for Him, we can see how His love and creativity are woven into every part of our lives.

God also reveals His glory in the athleticism of His creation. The incredible things athletes can do—jumping higher, running faster, lifting heavier, or performing feats that seem almost impossible—showcase the creativity and brilliance of the God who made us. It's mind-blowing to think that the same God who created the stars and oceans also created each of us with unique abilities and talents. When we use those abilities to their fullest, we reflect His glory to the world.

Look at your team. The way each person plays a role, supports one another, and works toward a shared goal reflects something much deeper than just strategy—it reflects the relational nature of God. Just as the Father, Son, and Holy Spirit live in perfect unity, your team can model that same kind of connection when it functions with humility, trust, and shared purpose.

The next time you step onto the field, the court, or the gym, pause and look around. Feel the breeze, hear the sounds, and recognize that the Creator of the universe is right there with you—*"The Lord your God is with you, the Mighty Warrior who saves. He will take great delight in you"* (Zephaniah 3:17)—cheering you on, strengthening you, and shaping you into who He's called you to be. When you start to see God in everything, it changes your perspective and deepens your connection with Him.

Reflection Question

How can you train yourself to see God's presence in the ordinary moments of your athletic and daily life?

— Coach Dickinson

48

Life of Faith

**"Jesus said: Your faith has saved you; go in peace."
— Luke 7:50**

The district championship. The biggest game of Michael's life. The pressure was real—college coaches watching, his future at Wake Forest on the line. This was his moment.

But then—disaster. Six interceptions. Each one felt like a gut punch, a weight pressing heavier on his chest. He could see it in his team-mates' eyes, feel it in the way the crowd murmured. And worst of all, that Wake Forest coach had a front-row seat to the worst game of his career.

The doubt crept in fast. **You blew it. You're not good enough.** Shame whispered in his ear, trying to take hold. It would've been easy to believe the lies, to let one game define him.

But Michael had a choice.

Instead of drowning in failure, he turned to something stronger—his faith. He knew Jesus never called the perfect; He called the willing. Michael remembered what mattered most: **his**

identity wasn't in his performance but in God's grace. One game didn't change his worth. One failure didn't cancel his purpose.

The enemy wanted him stuck in shame, but Michael wasn't having it. He let go of the guilt and clung to truth—**he was created by God, redeemed by Christ, and nothing could separate him from that love.**

The game was over, but Michael's journey wasn't. He walked off the field, head held high, knowing faith wasn't about avoiding failure—it was about rising after it. He knew the road ahead wouldn't always be easy, but he was ready not **just for college football but for life.** Because real confidence doesn't come from stats or scholarships—it comes from knowing who you are in Christ.

Reflection Question

How can your relationship with Jesus help you move past tough times?

— **Coach Diso**

49

What is a Promise?

"God is not a man, that He should lie, nor a son of man, that He should change His mind. Does He speak and then not act? Does He promise and not fulfill?" — Numbers 23:19 (NIV)

A promise is more than just words—it's a commitment, a bond, an expectation. In sports and life, we make promises all the time. A coach promises to push his players to be their best. Teammates promise to show up, work hard, and have each other's backs. Athletes promise themselves that they'll train, improve, and never quit. Friends promise to keep a secret. Boyfriends and girlfriends make promises of staying together forever.

And when they do, it hurts. In sports, broken promises can damage trust faster than a losing streak. Maybe a teammate bails when you need them most, or a coach says they'll play you and never follows through. These moments can leave scars—and skepticism. It becomes harder to believe others and even harder to believe that God will keep His word. But unlike people, God is *always* faithful. His consistency heals what human inconsistency breaks.

That kind of follow-through matters. As athletes, when we keep our word—even when it's hard—we reflect the character of a God who never fails. Whether committing to off-season workouts, staying loyal to teammates, or showing up with a good attitude when things don't go your way, your faithfulness says something. You become someone others can trust. And when your reliability points back to God's, that's powerful.

When God makes a promise, He keeps it. **Always. Without fail. Without exception**.

God promises to be with us in every challenge (*Deuteronomy 31:6*), to give us strength when we feel weak (*Isaiah 40:31*), and to give us His peace when we are anxious (*John 14:27*). He promises to provide for our needs (*Philippians 4:19*), to give us wisdom when we ask (*James 1:5*), to forgive us when we confess our sins (*1 John 1:9*), **and—miraculously—to forget our sin once we have been forgiven** (*Hebrews 8:12*).

I remember a time when I promised my players we'd fight until the last whistle, no matter the score. That game was brutal. Down by double digits, everything seemed lost. But we did not quit. We dug in and played with heart, and even though we didn't win on the scoreboard, we honored our promise never to give up.

It was a win for our integrity.

God's promises are like that—but even better. He doesn't just promise to show up; He guarantees victory (*1 Corinthians 15:57*). It may not always look like what we expect, but He never fails.

Even at its best, a promise is made with good intentions in this world—but it can still fall short. At worst, it's a hopeful commitment that may not always be kept.

With God, a promise is a certainty.

He promises that He is working all things for our good (*Romans 8:28*), that He hears our prayers (*1 John 5:14*), and that eternal life is ours through Christ (*1 John 2:25*).

Reflection Question

Which of God's promises do you need to hold on to today? How can you actively live in faith, trusting in His faithfulness?

— Coach Dickinson

50

Freedom

"It is for freedom that Christ has set us free." — 2 Corinthians 3:17

Letting down a coach is one of the hardest things an athlete can experience. I still remember the gut-wrenching feeling of failing a class or making a costly mistake in a game—the way my coach's disappointed look cut deep, like a spotlight on my short-comings. In those moments, I felt I wasn't enough; my mistakes defined me more than my potential.

But then, there were coaches who didn't just correct me—they lifted me up. They reminded me that failure wasn't the final chapter. Their belief in me gave me a sense of freedom, releasing me from the weight of my own doubts. As I grew, I realized that this kind of freedom—the freedom to move forward, grow, and not be held hostage by failure—was exactly what Jesus offers us.

In Christ, freedom means we are no longer chained to our past mistakes. It means we have the power to choose—to say no to the things that pull us away from God and yes to a life filled with purpose and love. With Jesus, we don't have to stay stuck in our failures or disappointments. He gives us the freedom to get back up, shake off the weight of guilt, and step into the life God has for us.

Jesus is the perfect example of what it looks like to live in that freedom. He walked in love, grace, and peace, showing us that when we lean on Him, we don't have to carry the burden of our past. Whenever we feel like we're falling short, we have a choice—to turn to Him and find the freedom that only He can give.

Real freedom isn't about having no struggles but knowing that we're never alone in them. It's about stepping out of the darkness of shame and into the light of Christ, where hope and clarity thrive. So, as you move forward, remember this: you are not your mistakes. With Jesus leading the way, you have the strength to rise, to grow, and to walk confidently toward the incredible life God has for you. In Him, you are truly free.

Reflection Questions

1. Think of a time when you let down your coach—what did you learn from it?

2. What is something Jesus can set you free from today?

— Coach Diso

51

This Too Shall Pass

"For our light and momentary troubles are achieving for us an eternal glory that far outweighs them all. So we fix our eyes not on what is seen, but on what is unseen, since what is seen is temporary, but what is unseen is eternal." — 2 Corinthians 4:17-18

The phrase *"This too shall pass"* has an uncertain origin, but I remember the first time I heard it—I didn't like it. In fact, I was offended. I was going through something difficult, and someone had the nerve to tell me my pain—my struggle—was only temporary? It felt like they were dismissing what I was feeling at that moment.

My dad had his way of making the same point. At times, when I was upset about something, he would ask, *"What will this matter a year from now?"* If I fired back, he'd ask, *"What will it matter two years from now?"* And if I still insisted it was a big deal, he'd say, *"What about ten years from now?"* Eventually, I started to understand what he was getting at. He wasn't saying my feelings didn't matter—he was helping me step back and see the bigger picture.

In sports, in life, and in our faith journey, **perspective is everything**. We go through seasons of highs and lows in competition and life. Struggles are inevitable, and as Christians, we're not just promised challenges—we are called to endure suffering at times. There will be moments when it feels like the weight of the world is pressing down on us. But here's the truth: most of what we're anxious about today **won't define our future**. The hard times won't last forever, and the pain we experience now will eventually give way to something greater.

The world tells us that happiness is the goal, defining it by temporary success, comfort, and achievement. But happiness isn't a destination—it's a perspective. When we fix our eyes on what is temporary, we end up chasing something just out of reach. But when we focus on what is eternal—on God's promises—we discover a peace that sustains us through every season.

So when life feels overwhelming, when the struggle feels too heavy, remember this:

This too shall pass. But more importantly, **God remains in control**. And when we trust Him, we can walk through any storm with confidence, knowing He is working all things for our good.

Reflection Question

What are you going through right now that feels overwhelming? How can shifting your perspective help you find peace in the middle of the storm?

— Coach Dickinson

52

Win Big

"My life is worth nothing to me unless I use it for finishing the work assigned me by the Lord Jesus—the work of telling others the good news about the wonderful grace of God."
— Acts 20:24

When I first met Deondre as a freshman, he was walking a tightrope between potential and self-destruction. Life hadn't been easy for him. He had the drive—the dream of playing college football—but the obstacles stacked against him were enough to make most people quit. Teachers and past coaches had already written him off, saying he wouldn't even graduate. His future? According to them, it wasn't looking too bright.

But standing in the gap was his mother—a force of unwavering love and sacrifice. She believed in him when few others did, doing everything in her power to give him a shot at something better.

That's when I stepped in not just with a game plan for football but with a bigger plan—one built on faith. Deondre had to take a leap, trust the process, and believe there was more for him than the world had decided. And man, did he rise to the challenge.

By his senior year, Deondre was unstoppable. He broke records, made plays that had recruiters turning their heads, and proved every doubter wrong. But when the season ended, uncertainty crept in. What was next? Was he truly ready for the next chapter?

See, trusting in Jesus can feel like stepping off a ledge. The world tells us to control everything, to hold on tight, to make sure we have all the answers before we move. But real faith? It's about surrender. It's about believing that when we let go, God's got us. And when He's got us, we don't just win—we win big.

I told Deondre that sometimes losing control is the first thing leading to true freedom. **Proverbs 3:6 says it beautifully:** *"In all your ways submit to Him, and He will make your paths straight."* When we surrender our fears, doubts, and plans to God, we make room for something greater—something beyond what we could ever build on our own. The world tells us we have to earn love, prove our worth, and fight for approval. But Jesus? He flips that script. His love isn't earned—it's given. His grace isn't based on performance—it's unconditional.

Deondre embraced that truth. And because of it, his story didn't end where others predicted. He went on to play college ball, yes—but more importantly, he walked across that stage with a diploma in hand, defying every expectation placed on him. His success wasn't just about the game; it was about his faith, his perseverance, and his willingness to trust in a God who had bigger plans than anyone could see.

That's the power of faith. When we lean into Jesus, our lives take on a new purpose—one that no circumstance, failure, or doubt can take away. Deondre's story is proof that no matter how tough the road, God's plan is always bigger, always better, and always worth trusting. So whatever battle you're facing, whatever doubt is creeping in—turn it over to Him. Because when God's in your corner, you're already set up to win.

Reflection Questions

1. Think of a time when someone stepped in and helped you through a tough season. How did it change you?

2. What's one thing you need to surrender to Jesus today?

— Coach Diso

53

When Only Jesus Is Enough

"When Jesus saw their faith, he said, 'Friend, your sins are forgiven.'" — Luke 5:20

In Luke 5, we read about a paralytic man whose friends brought him to Jesus. They carried him through the crowds, up onto the roof, and lowered him into Peter's house. These friends did everything they could to help, but they understood their limitations: They couldn't heal him—only Jesus could.

When Jesus saw their faith, He forgave the man's sins and then healed him, saying, "I tell you, get up, take your mat, and go home" (Luke 5:24). The man's complete restoration testified to Christ's power to heal both spiritually and physically.

This story reminds us of a humbling truth: "I am not the Christ." While I can reflect Christ and love others through Him, only He has the power to heal, forgive, and transform lives. These friends' faith wasn't just in their efforts but in Christ's ability to deliver what was needed.

As athletes, we've all faced moments when we've leaned on our teammates to support us—whether it's finishing a tough practice, executing a game plan, or lifting each other's spirits after a tough loss. Great teammates know when to step in and encourage you, but they also know when they can best point you back to your training or coach for guidance.

Similarly, in life, there have been many times students and athletes have come to me seeking help, direction, or advice. During these moments, I actively listen and draw on the Holy Spirit to guide what I might say. Sometimes, I have a story or experience that helps bring clarity. Other times, I simply offer to pray with them, inviting God into the conversation. I've found that praying—especially together—connects us not only to each other but to Christ's power. And when I don't have the words, I've realized that simply pointing them to Jesus is often the greatest help I can give.

Life offers challenges designed to bring us closer to the Savior—the One who knows our problems and the answers to them before we even ask. During these times, true Christian friends admit, "I don't know, but I know who does," and point us back to Jesus, often offering a prayer to guide and comfort us.

No matter how much preparation you've done on game day, the responsibility to take the shot, make the play, or execute the strategy ultimately falls to you. Your teammates and coaches can support you, but there are moments when you're alone with the ball or the goal, and you have to rely on something bigger. Life works the same way. We can lean on others, but only Jesus can meet our deepest needs and provide true healing and peace.

Reflection Questions

1. Who are the friends in your life who point you to Jesus?

2. How can you be the kind of friend who helps carry others closer to Christ?

3. What is one way you can encourage a teammate or friend to trust Jesus this week?

— Coach Dickinson

54

The Voice

"My sheep listen to my voice; I know them, and they follow me." — John 10:27

In any team sport, the captain plays a pivotal role. They're the ones at midfield for the coin toss, leading the huddle in crucial moments, and often the only players the officials communicate with during a game. A captain's job isn't just about wearing a title—it's about relaying the coach's expectations, setting the tone, and leading with conviction. Leadership in sports is built on trust and communication. The best captains don't just talk; they listen. They recognize the importance of hearing their coach's voice, absorbing their instructions, and executing the game plan.

It's no different in life. Every great leader listens to a voice that guides them—whether it's a coach, mentor, or trusted friend. But for Christians, the most important voice we can listen to isn't coming from the sidelines or a locker room; it's the voice of the Holy Spirit.

Just as athletes rely on their coaches for direction, we are called to lean on the Holy Spirit for guidance, encouragement, and discipline. In the Old Testament, God spoke in powerful ways—He called Moses from a burning bush and sent angels to deliver His messages. When Jesus walked the earth, God's voice became even more personal. He was the living Word, teaching and leading His disciples face to face. But before returning to Heaven, Jesus made a promise: He would send a Helper to continue guiding His followers. That Helper is the Holy Spirit.

The moment we accept Jesus as our Savior, the Holy Spirit takes residence in our lives. He doesn't shout through a loudspeaker or send text messages—He speaks directly to our hearts. He is always there, whether we're in the middle of a tough decision, wrestling with doubt, or celebrating a victory. Even in moments of loneliness, we are never truly alone.

Just like a captain who listens to their coach to lead the team, we must listen to the Holy Spirit to navigate life. God is always present through Him, guiding us through every peak and valley, ensuring we are never without His wisdom, strength, and love. The question isn't whether God is speaking—the question is whether we are listening.

Reflection Questions

1. Who is an important voice or role model in your life that you trust for guidance?

2. How does it change your perspective to know the Holy Spirit is always with you, guiding and leading you?

— Coach Diso

55

Timeless Wisdom from the Wisest King

"The fear of the LORD is the beginning of knowledge, but fools despise wisdom and instruction."
— Proverbs 1:7

When I was in high school, I was searching for wisdom—something solid to guide me. I already knew about the Book of Proverbs, but it wasn't until I truly started reading and applying it that I realized how powerful it was. These short, impactful sayings weren't just good advice—they were timeless truths, packed into single verses or small sections, meant to shape every stage of life.

The book of Proverbs is primarily written by King Solomon, the son of David, who is known as the wisest king to ever live (1 Kings 3:5–12). God granted Solomon extraordinary wisdom, which is recorded in this book.

In my immaturity, I put these words to the test. Sometimes, I listened and applied them. Other times, I ignored them and learned through painful experiences. I remember one season where I trained all summer for a starting spot but slacked off once I got it. My coach benched me within weeks—not out of spite, but to teach discipline. That moment hit hard. Proverbs warned me ("The complacency of fools will destroy them," 1:32), and I lived it the hard way. Looking back, I wish I had chosen wisdom more often. My hope is that you will choose the better path.

There's a deep connection between athletic discipline and spiritual discipline. Both require daily commitment, humility, and a willingness to be coached. Like running drills shape your body, absorbing Proverbs trains your heart and mind in godly wisdom.

Here's my challenge to you: read **one proverb a day**. Pair it with your daily devotion and reflect on how it applies to your life. Let these verses **guide your walk with Christ**.

"Trust in the LORD with all your heart and lean not on your own understanding; in all your ways submit to him, and he will make your paths straight." — Proverbs 3:5-6

"Above all else, guard your heart, for everything you do flows from it." — Proverbs 4:23

"Hatred stirs up conflict, but love covers over all wrongs." — Proverbs 10:12

"When pride comes, then comes disgrace, but with humility comes wisdom." — Proverbs 11:2

"Whoever loves discipline loves knowledge, but whoever hates correction is stupid." — Proverbs 12:1

"Walk with the wise and become wise, for a companion of fools suffers harm." — Proverbs 13:20

"There is a way that appears to be right, but in the end, it leads to death." — Proverbs 14:12

"A gentle answer turns away wrath, but a harsh word stirs up anger." — Proverbs 15:1

"Pride goes before destruction, a haughty spirit before a fall." — Proverbs 16:18

"A cheerful heart is good medicine, but a crushed spirit dries up the bones." — Proverbs 17:22

"The tongue has the power of life and death, and those who love it will eat its fruit." — Proverbs 18:21

"If your enemy is hungry, give him food to eat; if he is thirsty, give him water to drink. In doing this, you will heap burning coals on his head, and the LORD will reward you." — Proverbs 25:21-22

"As iron sharpens iron, so one person sharpens another." — Proverbs 27:17

Reflection Question

Which proverb stands out to you the most today? How can you apply it to your life?

— Coach Dickinson

56

Work

"And we know that in all things God works for the good of those who love him, who have been called according to his purpose." — Romans 8:28

When I was in high school, my dream was singular—to become a professional athlete. I put in the hours, the effort, and the extra reps when no one was watching. I pushed myself beyond what others were willing to do, determined to separate myself from the pack. But no matter how hard I worked, I was never the standout player. I faced setback after setback—coaching changes, injuries, and the reality of competing against All-American athletes ahead of me on the depth chart. Sometimes, it felt like I was pouring everything into a dream that wasn't meant to happen.

But here's the truth I didn't fully understand back then: **God wastes nothing.**

He is always working, even when we don't see it. He doesn't sit back and let things unfold—He is active in every struggle, every challenge, every moment of our lives. And just as God is constantly at work, we are called to do the same. Faith isn't passive. It requires action, a fire within us that compels us to grow, serve, and pursue a deeper relationship with Christ.

God doesn't call us to sit on the sidelines. He calls us to get in the game—to trust Him in the grind, to put in the work, and to keep going even when we don't see immediate results. Through the ups and downs, I kept pushing. I trained. I sacrificed. I worked relentlessly. I can see that God never wasted a single moment. Every challenge, every ounce of effort, every frustrating setback was preparing me for something bigger. The rewards weren't just about wins or stats; they were about perseverance, faith, and learning to trust God's timing over my own.

In many ways, that journey shaped me into someone who walks with others through their struggles and growth. When you've been refined in the fire, you're better equipped to lead with empathy, patience, and purpose. Your leadership becomes less about control and more about service—less about outcomes and more about the people you're called to pour into.

You might be in a season right now where you're questioning if the work is worth it. Let me remind you—**it is.** Stay faithful. Stay in the fight. Because the God who called you is working in every step, shaping you for something greater than you can imagine.

Reflection Questions

1. What are you working toward today?

2. Is your effort—whether in practice, training, or daily life—honoring God?

— Coach Diso

57

Just in Time

"He has made everything beautiful in its time. He has also set eternity in the human heart; yet no one can fathom what God has done from beginning to end." — Ecclesiastes 3:11 (NIV)

In sports, timing is everything. A perfectly timed pass can lead to a game-winning shot. A sprinter's start off the blocks determines their finish. A baseball player's swing must connect at just the right moment. No matter how much skill an athlete has, the play falls apart if the timing is off.

Life often feels the same way. We work, prepare, and pray—but sometimes, things don't happen when we expect them to. We wonder if God has forgotten about us, if our prayers are unheard, or if our dreams will ever become reality. But just like in sports, God's timing is never random; it is always perfect.

Look at the story of Lazarus (John 11:1-44). Mary and Martha begged Jesus to come to heal their brother. But Jesus delayed, and by the time He arrived, Lazarus had been dead for four days. To them, it was too late. But Jesus knew otherwise. Instead of just healing a sick man, He raised a dead one—proving that God's timing always brings a greater purpose.

Or take Joseph's journey (Genesis 37-50). He was sold into slavery, falsely accused, and imprisoned. It took years before he saw God's plan unfold. But when it did, Joseph was in the perfect position to save his family and an entire nation from famine. What seemed like a series of disappointments was actually a divine setup.

Maybe you're in a season of waiting. Perhaps you feel like God's answer is taking too long. This can be especially hard for athletes—waiting through an injury, recovering from a setback, or sitting on the bench when you're desperate to contribute. But here's the truth: God is never early and never late. He's always right on time. His delays are not denials—they are preparations for something better.

What feels like a pause might actually be His way of strengthening your character, deepening your trust, and preparing you for what's next. Instead of growing impatient, what if you shifted your perspective? What if, instead of frustration, you responded with faith? What if, instead of waiting with doubt, you trusted with expectation?

Reflection Question

Think of a time when something in your life didn't happen when you expected it to, but later, you saw God's perfect timing. How can you trust Him in your current season of waiting?

— Coach Dickinson

58

All-In

**"You must love the Lord your God with all your
heart, soul, mind, and strength." — Mark 12:30**

B eing "all in" on your team isn't just about showing up—it's
about committing with everything you've got. It's easy to give
effort when you're getting something in return—when your teammates support you, when your coaches recognize your hard work,
when everything is clicking. But true commitment isn't a transac-
tion. It's a choice. It's choosing to serve your team even when no
one is watching, to lift others up even when it doesn't benefit you,
and to stay locked in when it would be easier to check out. The
moments I cherish most—both as a player and a coach—weren't
about my success. They were the moments I put others first.

Our relationship with Jesus is no different. He doesn't ask for part of
our hearts. He calls us to be *all in*—to love Him with everything we
have: heart, soul, mind, and strength. That means more than just
knowing about Him. It's about fully surrendering to Him, allowing
His presence in our lives to shape our emotions, thoughts, and
actions.

God understands every emotion we experience—joy, sorrow, trust, frustration, excitement—because we were created in His image. Our emotions aren't random; they are a reflection of our Creator. But just like in sports, emotions need to be trained. It's easy to let frustration, anger, or doubt dictate our actions, but real strength comes from trusting God even when our emotions try to take over.

Worship isn't just about singing songs on Sunday—it's about bringing every emotion, every victory, and every struggle to Him and letting His Spirit guide us through it. Let your life show others that trusting God with every emotion is where real freedom and strength are found. Lead with authenticity, and others will follow—not because you have all the answers, but because you're walking closely with the One who does.

Being "all in" means fully committing to your faith, your team, and the calling God has placed on your life. It's about showing up, serving, and trusting that God is working through every moment, whether it's a win or a tough loss. When we live this way, we don't just impact ourselves—we create a legacy that inspires others to do the same. So, are you *all in*?

Reflection Questions

1. What would it look like for you to be *all in*—in your faith, relationships, and commitments?

2. How could shifting your mindset to being *all in* bring you closer to God?

— Coach Diso

59

So Close, but So Far Away

"There is a way that appears to be right, but in the end, it leads to death." — Proverbs 14:12 (NIV)

Have you ever watched a shot bounce off the rim at the buzzer? Have you seen a runner stretch for the finish line only to fall inches short? Maybe you've watched a putt roll toward the hole, only to lip out at the last second. So close—but not close enough.

Many people approach life—and eternity—the same way. They assume they'll be fine as long as they're a "good person" by the world's standards. They think if they work hard, treat others well, and avoid major mistakes, they're on the right path. But the truth is, being "good" isn't good enough when measured by God's standard.

The world defines goodness in relative terms—comparing one person's actions to another's. One person might say, "I'm a good person because I don't lie." Another might say, "I'm not perfect, but at least I'm not as bad as that guy." But God doesn't grade on a curve. His standard isn't just better—it's perfect (Matthew 5:48).

Look at the story of the rich young ruler (Mark 10:17–27). He had everything—wealth, influence, and a reputation for keeping God's commandments. By human standards, he was a great guy. In many ways, he's like a top athlete who's always been praised, never really had to ask for help, and believes their success proves their worth. But excellence without surrender can become a trap. When Jesus told him to sell his possessions and follow Him, the young man walked away sad—because he was unwilling to give up what truly ruled his heart. He was so close, but he missed it. His goodness wasn't enough—he needed surrender.

Many people face this reality. They try to live a good life, but without Jesus, they miss the mark. Romans 3:23 reminds us, "For all have sinned and fall short of the glory of God." No matter how much effort we put in, we can't reach perfection on our own. The only way to truly "win" in the game of life is not by being good but by being transformed from the inside out by Jesus' love and forgiveness.

Maybe you've been relying on your own goodness instead of God's grace. Maybe you've thought that God will accept you if you just do enough. But the good news is this: You don't have to earn your way to Him—Jesus already paid the price. The question is: Will you accept it?

Reflection Question

Are you measuring your life by the world's definition of good or by God's standard? Have you truly surrendered to Jesus, or are you just hoping that "good enough" will be enough?

— Coach Dickinson

60

God Controls All

"The Lord will save me." — Isaiah 38:20

H unger isn't just about food. We hunger for connection, purpose, and understanding. We chase goals, relationships, and
opportunities, hoping to fill something inside us. And sometimes,
we don't realize how much God is working in those moments until
we look back.

One day, I had some leftover concession stand pizza sitting on my
desk. Before I could even think about which players to give it to, it
vanished. A quick investigation led me straight to the culprit—Manasee—his guilty face smeared with pizza sauce like undeniable evidence. That season, Manasee struggled. Injuries, discipline issues,
fights, and now, adding theft to the list. Eventually, those struggles
led to his removal from the team. Shortly after, my own career took
me to another school, and I never got the chance to speak to him
again.

Then, a decade later, he walked through my office door.

Surprise doesn't even begin to describe what I felt. *Do you remember me?* he asked, uncertainty in his voice. I smiled, stood up, and pulled him in for a hug. In an instant, all the memories came back—his struggles, the tough conversations, the discipline, and the moments I had to hold him accountable. But in that reunion, something unexpected happened. We exchanged apologies. He apologized for the challenges he had brought to me and the team. And I apologized for how I had enforced discipline without always giving him the perspective behind it.

Manasee had changed. He wasn't the same kid who stole a slice of pizza and made my job harder. He was standing in front of me as a man—seeking a coaching internship, ready to mentor young athletes the same way I once mentored him. He wanted to hold players to the same standards of accountability that had once shaped him. That moment wasn't just about reconnecting—it was about redemption.

God had been working in his life the entire time.

Today, Manasse is out there inspiring athletes, holding them accountable, and leading with integrity. Luke 21:28 tells us to "stand up and lift your heads because your redemption is drawing near." And every time I think about him, I'm reminded: **accountability breeds growth, faith fuels resilience, and every struggle can be the foundation of an incredible redemption story**.

Too often, we go through difficult circumstances and see them as roadblocks, setbacks, or failures. But when we look at them through the eyes of faith, we begin to see something different—possibility. The struggles that seem overwhelming today may be shaping us for something greater tomorrow.

I've seen firsthand how God takes broken situations and turns them into powerful testimonies. He doesn't just leave us in the struggle—He redeems, restores, and transforms. Even when we can't see it, **God is in control.**

Reflection Questions

1. What situation in your life do you need God to intervene in?

2. Have you ever experienced a moment of redemption? How did it change you?

—Coach Diso

61

Who Loves More?

"Therefore, I tell you, her many sins have been forgiven—as her great love has shown. But whoever has been forgiven little loves little." — Luke 7:47

There's something powerful about realizing just how much grace has been poured out on your life. In Luke 7, Jesus tells the Parable of the Two Debtors to a Pharisee named Simon. One debtor owed a small amount, the other a much larger sum, but both were forgiven completely. Jesus asks, "Which of them will love him more?" Simon answers, "The one who had the bigger debt forgiven."

Now, compare that to the Parable of the Prodigal Son (Luke 15). The younger son took his inheritance, wasted it all, and hit rock bottom. When he returned home, expecting judgment, he instead found his father running to embrace him with open arms. His father didn't hesitate—he forgave him completely. And what was the son's response? Deep gratitude. Deep love.

Both Simon the Pharisee and the older brother in the Prodigal Son story had something in common—pride blinded them to their need for grace. They were so focused on their own righteousness that they couldn't see how much they needed forgiveness. And when we fail to see our sin, we struggle to appreciate the depth of God's love. Pride convinces us that grace is for "other people,"—but humility opens our hearts to receive it.

This truth isn't just found in Scripture; it plays out in everyday life. I remember when I was a kid, I was mowing our property with a tractor. My dad came home with a new truck, and I was so excited to see it that I got nervous when I approached. I hit the gas instead of the brake and rammed the driver's door, leaving a huge dent. My dad calmly reversed the tractor, grabbed a tool to start fixing the dent, and then put me back on the tractor to finish mowing. He never yelled. He never shamed me. He forgave me and moved on.

I never forgot how that whole situation made me feel. I was completely in the wrong, but I experienced grace.

Athletes get this on the field. Think about that moment when a coach gives you another chance after a mistake, when a teammate lifts you up after a failure, or when you win a game you didn't deserve to win. It changes you. When you experience grace, you want to play harder, fight stronger, and hopefully give that same grace to others.

God's grace is the ultimate game-changer. The more we recognize how much we've been forgiven, the more our love for Him deepens—and the more we extend that same grace to others.

Reflection Questions

1. Do you see yourself as someone who has been forgiven

much or little? How does that impact your love for God?

2. Have you ever struggled to celebrate when someone else received grace? Why?

3. Are you more like the prodigal son (grateful for grace) or the older brother (struggling to understand it)?

4. Who in your life needs grace today, and how can you show it to them?

— Coach Dickinson

62

Waiting

"He has made everything appropriate in its time. He also set eternity in their heart, yet so that man will not find out the work which God has done from the beginning even to the end." — Ecclesiastes 3:11

In sports, every moment counts. The spotlight shines on those who step up when their time comes. But what about the ones who wait? Waiting can feel like a test of endurance, a challenge to your confidence, and a battle against frustration.

Danny knew this feeling all too well. His chances of stepping onto the field were slim as a fourth-string player. He could have sulked, made excuses, or gone through the motions. But instead, he chose a different path. He committed to the grind. Every day, he trained like he was the starter, mentally and physically preparing himself—not because he was guaranteed an opportunity, but because he refused to be unprepared if one came.

And then, just before the season began, everything changed. A series of unexpected events forced him into the starting role. Some doubted him; others underestimated him. But he was ready. He didn't just step up—he dominated, shattering expectations and setting two school records in the process.

Danny's story is proof that **waiting isn't wasted time—it's preparation time.**

Too often, we see waiting as passive. But in reality, it's an active season where God is working, shaping, and refining us. Think about it: the miracle of birth takes nine months from conception to delivery. You don't rush the process—you trust that growth is happening, even when you can't see it. Our spiritual journey works the same way. **God's timing is never rushed, but it's always right.**

Waiting can be frustrating, especially when we feel like we have no control. But maybe that's the point. God invites us to let go of our need to control every outcome and to trust Him completely. **We don't wait because we have patience—we wait because we trust the One who holds the future.**

Danny's story reminds us that you don't want to step into your moment unprepared when the waiting season ends. The time you spend training, growing, and strengthening your faith isn't wasted—it's positioning you for something greater.

Are you using your waiting season to get ready?

Reflection Questions

1. What opportunities are you waiting or hoping for?

2. How can you use this time of waiting to grow in faith and preparation?

— Coach Diso

63

You Miss 100% of the Shots You Don't Take

"Then Peter got down out of the boat, walked on the water and came toward Jesus." — Matthew 14:29

Every athlete knows the fear of missing a shot. The pressure is real—what if you fail? What if you let your team down? What if the ball doesn't go in? But here's the truth: you guarantee failure if you never take the shot. The only way to have a chance at success is to step up and take it.

Peter learned this firsthand. When Jesus called him out of the boat, Peter had a decision to make—stay where it was safe or take the risk and step onto the water. He could have overthought it, let doubt creep in, and stayed put. But he didn't. He took the shot. And for a moment, he did the impossible—he walked on water!

Sure, Peter started sinking when he took his eyes off Jesus, but here's what we often forget: at least he got out of the boat. The other disciples stayed behind, too afraid to try. Peter was the one who experienced God's power in a way they never did—because he took the shot.

In life, fear will try to hold you back. Maybe God is calling you to step into leadership, start something new, or share your faith. Maybe you've been waiting for the "perfect moment" to take action. But if you never take the shot, you'll never see what God can do.

I remember when the head football coach called on me to be the JV head football coach. I certainly was not qualified. I doubted myself, questioned my ability, and almost let fear keep me on the sidelines. But he believed in me. And in that moment, I had a choice—stay in my comfort zone or take the shot. I took it. And looking back, if I hadn't stepped up, my relationship with Coach Diso might have never been. That single decision changed my life.

You don't have to feel ready. You just have to be willing. God isn't looking for the most qualified—He's looking for those who trust Him enough to step out of the boat. **Because real faith always shows up in action. As James 2:17 says, "Faith by itself, if it is not accompanied by action, is dead."** Peter didn't just believe Jesus could do the impossible—he acted on it. And that's what made the miracle possible.

So, what about you? Are you going to sit on the bench when God is calling you into the game? Step up. Take the shot. Trust Him with the outcome.

Reflection Question

What's one step of faith you've been afraid to take? What's holding you back?

— Coach Dickinson

64

Worthy of Praise

"Whatever is true, noble, right, pure, lovely, admirable—if anything is excellent or praiseworthy—think about such things." —Philippians 4:8

In sports, passion and pressure go hand in hand. I've seen it firsthand—athletes battling frustration, disappointment, and self-doubt. They come to me with their heads down, shoulders heavy, struggling with poor performance, conflicts with coaches, or division within the team. I get it. I've been there.

In those moments, I tell them something simple but powerful: *You can't change what's already happened, but you can control what you focus on.*

Your mind is a battleground. What you choose to dwell on shapes your perspective, attitude, and, ultimately, your ability to move forward. If mistakes, setbacks, or failures consume your thoughts, they'll weigh you down. But if you shift your focus and set your mind on what is true, noble, and praiseworthy, you open the door to growth, resilience, and hope.

That doesn't mean ignoring pain or pretending struggles don't exist. It means recognizing when negative thoughts start taking over and choosing to hand them over to Jesus. He never asked us to carry the weight of the past or to predict the future. That's His job. **Ours is to trust.**

I've learned that God sees me and walks with me—**always, even** when I don't feel it, even when my circumstances say otherwise. The ability to reset our thoughts and shift our perspective starts with trust, which is built one decision at a time.

The battle against negativity is won one thought at a time. When we actively choose to dwell on God's truth instead of leaning on our own understanding, we step into a new level of strength. We rise above frustration. We take back control of our mindset. We learn that setbacks are never final—they're just setups for something greater.

Reflection Questions

1. What are some challenging thoughts you need to hand over to Jesus today?

2. How can shifting your focus toward what is good and praiseworthy lead to different outcomes?

— Coach Diso

65

Who am I?

"I praise you because I am fearfully and wonderfully made; your works are wonderful, I know that full well." — Psalm 139:14

If you've ever put on a jersey, you know that identity matters. That name across your chest represents something bigger than you—your team, school, and community. It's a symbol of commitment, sacrifice, and pride. But what happens when the season ends? Who are you when the stadium lights go off and the crowd is gone?

I remember a player who gave everything to the game. He was the first to practice and the last to leave. But when an injury ended his career, he struggled. Without the sport, he felt like he had lost himself. He had spent years defining himself by a jersey—but that jersey didn't define who he truly was.

I've seen too many athletes wrestle with that question. They pour everything into their sport, investing their heart, time, and energy into being the best. And for a while, that's enough. But then an injury happens. Graduation comes. The sport that once defined them is suddenly no longer there. And when the thing they built their identity on is gone, they feel empty and lost.

But here's the truth: you are more than a jersey. More than a scoreboard. More than the wins and losses. If your worth is tied to performance, it will rise and fall with every game. But Psalm 139:14 reminds us of something deeper—we are fearfully and wonderfully made. Before you ever picked up a ball, ran a sprint, or stepped onto a field, God knew you. He saw your potential before the world gave you a number, a position, or a title.

Sports are a gift, a passion—but they're not your identity. Your identity is in Christ. As 2 Corinthians 5:17 says, *"If anyone is in Christ, he is a new creation. The old has gone; the new is here!"* That truth doesn't just apply when the season ends—it applies to every moment of competition. You can give your all on the field, train hard, and strive for excellence without losing sight of who you are. Because your worth isn't defined by stats or success—it's rooted in something eternal. You are a child of God, created intentionally, loved deeply, and valuable beyond performance. The Creator of the universe designed you with a purpose that outlasts any season, any game, any title.

So, who are you? You're not just an athlete. You're His. And that's a name you'll never have to take off. Because long after the final whistle blows, long after the stadium goes quiet, you still belong. You are still chosen. You are still His.

Reflection Question

When the game is over, where do you find your true identity?

— Coach Dickinson

66

Clarity

"And we know that in all things God works for the good of those who love him, who have been called according to his purpose."
— Romans 8:28

At some point, we've all been pushed to our limits—by a coach, a teacher, a parent, or even a teammate. That feeling where you think you can't take another step, where giving up seems easier than pressing on, or where you just want to prove someone wrong. It's a familiar moment, especially in sports. Athletes are constantly pushed to their breaking point, expected to rise to the occasion even when exhaustion takes over. And let's be real—it's hard. But here's the thing: those breaking-point moments? They're where real growth happens.

Life isn't much different. The more you take on—practices, school-work, relationships—the heavier the load gets. But the key to carrying that weight isn't in sheer willpower. It's in clarity—knowing who you are and why you're here. And the best way to find that? A real, growing relationship with Jesus.

Walking with Jesus isn't always comfortable. It stretches you. It forces you to step out in faith when things feel uncertain. It's like being on shaky ground but trusting that He's got you. And that's where clarity comes in. Because when you surrender—when you stop trying to force everything to go your way and start trusting His way—you find a peace and purpose that nothing else can give.

Letting go doesn't mean giving up. It means trusting that God's plan is bigger than yours. He sees the whole picture when all you see is the struggle. And when you trust Him and truly lean into His purpose for your life, you'll find clarity like never before.

Sports are a gift, a passion—but they're not your identity. Your identity is in Christ. You are a child of God, created intentionally, loved deeply, and valuable beyond performance. The Creator of the universe designed you with a purpose that outlasts any season, any game, any title. Having teammates to support you through your journey not only helps you grow - but also reflects the heart of Jesus, who walked with His disciples through every storm and taught us to carry one another's burdens. As James 1:2–4 reminds us, trials produce perseverance, and with Christ at the center, we grow into maturity together.

So, who are you? You're not just an athlete. You are His. And that's a name you'll never have to take off. Because long after the final whistle blows, long after the stadium grows quiet, you still belong. You are still chosen. You are still His.

Reflection Questions

1. Where in your life do you feel like you're being stretched too thin?

2. How can stepping out of your comfort zone and surrender-

ing control to God help you find clarity and purpose in your challenges?

— Coach Diso

67

Don't Make a Decision Until You Have To

"But those who wait on the Lord shall renew their strength; they shall mount up with wings like eagles, they shall run and not be weary, they shall walk and not faint." — Isaiah 40:31

It was the fourth quarter of a tight game, and we had the ball with less than a minute left. The pressure was on. I had a timeout in my pocket, and my assistant coach leaned over and asked, "Coach, what's the call?"

I looked at him and said, **"I don't know yet."**

He gave me a puzzled look. The crowd was roaring, the clock was ticking, and he expected an immediate answer. But I wasn't about to make a decision before I had to. Why? Because I needed all the information I could get before making the best possible choice.

Athletes often feel pressured to make quick decisions about their future—choosing a college, transferring schools, orpicking a major. The reality? Most of the time, **you don't have to decide right away.** The key is to gather information, seek wise counsel, and pray—not just once but continually. Prayer is how we surrender control and invite the Holy Spirit to guide us. It doesn't always bring instant answers, but it does bring peace—and that peace can be your compass. When clarity doesn't come right away, it's okay. Wait. God is rarely in a hurry, but He's always on time.

More importantly, making a hasty decision can pull you out of alignment with God's plan. **His timing is perfect—never early, never late, always right on time.** When we force a decision out of fear or impatience, we risk missing the blessing He is preparing for us. What if God is using the waiting period to grow you, shape you, or align circumstances for something better than you imagined?

Here's what I've learned: When you feel rushed, that's often a sign to slow down. Urgency can cloud wisdom. Unless it's truly a crisis—like a game clock winding down—most decisions don't need to be made immediately. Ask yourself: *Is this decision urgent or just loud?* Pause. Pray. Let God settle your heart. When you invite Him into the process, His peace often gives you a sense of when to move and when to wait.

That night on the field, I waited just a little longer before calling the timeout. That extra time allowed me to see the defense's setup and make the right call. We ran the play and scored a touchdown. Had I panicked and rushed my decision, we wouldn't have scored. **Trust the process. Trust God.** Don't make a decision until you have to—so you don't get ahead of Him. When the moment comes, make the call with confidence, knowing you've sought wisdom, gathered information, and waited on His perfect timing.

Reflection Question

Is there a situation in your life where you are rushing ahead instead of waiting on God's perfect timing? How can you surrender it to Him today?

— Coach Dickinson

68

Declare What is True

"If you declare with your mouth, 'Jesus is Lord,' and believe in your heart that God raised him from the dead, you will be saved."
— Romans 10:9

Doubt is a battle we all fight. It sneaks in when we're struggling, when the pressure is on, or when things don't go as planned. Maybe you've questioned a decision, doubted your abilities after a bad game, or wondered if you're even on the right path. It happens. And let's be honest—the voices around us don't always help. A tough critique from a coach, a harsh comment from a teammate, or even our negative thoughts can leave us feeling stuck and unsure of what's next.

But in those moments, you must lock in on what is true. No matter how you feel, one thing doesn't change—**Jesus loves you just as you are.** That's not up for debate. It's not based on performance, approval, or success. Genesis 1:27 says, *"So God created mankind in His own image."* That means your worth isn't something you earn—it's something God already gave you. You were designed, on purpose, by the Creator of the universe. That truth is unshakable.

And here's something even bigger—God's love isn't something you can win or lose. It's already yours. John 3:16 makes it clear: *"For God so loved the world that He gave His one and only Son."* That love is sacrificial, permanent, and powerful. It doesn't change based on how well you play, how many times you mess up, or how much doubt you carry.

So when the challenging moments hit—when practice feels impossible, when the game slips away when criticism stings—stand firm in these truths:

- **I am enough because I am a child of God.**

- **I rejoice in suffering because Christ suffered for me**

- **I am not ashamed of Jesus because His sacrifice changes lives.**

- **I am greatly loved, so I love others as I have been loved.**

- **Nothing can separate me from God's love.**

These aren't just feel-good phrases — they're reality. When you declare them, you remind yourself of who you are. Christ suffered for you — taking your sin, your shame, your separation — so you could stand in freedom, be forgiven, and be fully loved. Because of Him, your identity is secure. No game, person, or failure can take away what God has already spoken over you. Walk in that truth today.

Reflection Questions

1. How can you remind yourself of your worth and identity in Christ during moments of doubt or failure?

2. How can you encourage someone struggling with self-doubt or negativity, helping them remember they are deeply loved and valued by God?

— Coach Diso

69

What is Camaraderie?

"As iron sharpens iron, so one person sharpens another." — Proverbs 27:17 (NIV)

The word *camaraderie* comes from the Latin *camera*, meaning "chamber" or "room." It evolved from the French word *camarade*, referring to a group of soldiers sharing the same quarters. At its core, camaraderie is about close friendship, trust, and unity among those who share a mission or goal.

Camaraderie isn't just about being teammates; it's about forming bonds beyond the game. It's about fighting challenges together, pushing each other to improve, and knowing that you're not alone.

When I think about camaraderie, I remember my years coaching with Coach Neff while Coach Diso was in high school. Those years shaped my character and played a key role in defining who I would become. Though they were centered around sports, they were ultimately about something much bigger—navigating the struggles of life, searching for purpose, and growing together in our walk with Jesus.

Think about the best teams you've ever participated in—on the field, in the locker room, or beyond. Were they the most talented? Maybe. But what truly set them apart was unity, trust, and how they sharpened each other. And that camaraderie doesn't have to end when the season does. Some of the closest friendships in my life are with former teammates and coaches. True connection, built on faith and shared purpose, endures beyond the game.

Just as the best teams thrive on trust and sacrifice, our faith journey is also meant to be shared. Hebrews 10:24-25 urges us to "consider how we may spur one another on toward love and good deeds... encouraging one another—and all the more as you see the Day approaching." We weren't meant to walk this journey alone. Faith is a team sport; fellowship keeps us sharp, accountable, and encouraged.

On the field and in faith, camaraderie is built through shared struggle, sacrifice, and encouragement. Sacrifice might mean giving up your starting spot so a teammate can shine, staying late to help someone recover from an injury, or putting your personal stats aside to do what's best for the team. It's choosing to put others ahead of yourself, to lift them when they're down, and to allow them to do the same for you. That kind of love reflects Christ.

Proverbs 27:17 reminds us that just as iron sharpens iron, we are meant to challenge and refine one another. That sharpening might look like a teammate calling you out when your effort slips in practice or a friend asking how your faith is holding up during a hard season. It could be staying after to help a teammate improve or having a hard but honest conversation that helps both of you grow. True camaraderie isn't passive—it's intentional, uncomfortable sometimes, and always worth it.

This week, be intentional about building camaraderie—both in your team and your faith. Encourage, challenge, and sharpen those around you. **Who can you uplift today?**

Reflection Question

How can you strengthen camaraderie with your teammates and in your walk with Christ this week?

— Coach Dickinson

70

Break Through

"See, I am doing a new thing! Now it springs up, do you not perceive it? I am making a way." — Isaiah 43:19

Injuries are a brutal part of an athlete's journey. They come out of nowhere—during training, in the middle of a game, or even near the end of a career. And it's not just the physical pain that hurts; it's the mental and emotional toll that can be even tougher to deal with. When an athlete goes down, it's not just about recovery but identity, purpose, and faith.

I saw this up close with Matt, one of the hardest-working athletes I'd ever coached. His senior season was supposed to be *the* season. He had put in the work, the hours, the sweat leading up to this moment. But two days before it all began, an injury took him out. Just like that, everything changed. It was devastating—for him, for me, for the entire team.

But in that broken moment, something new started. Through a log of tough conversations, Matt began to see things differently. We talked about how sometimes God allows setbacks to create setups. We don't always see it at the moment, but looking back, it becomes clear — He's shaping us, refining us, preparing us for something bigger. Like Romans 8:28 says, *"And we know that in all things God works for the good of those who love Him, who have been called according to His purpose."*

For Matt, that *"something bigger"* came when he stepped into a new role — as a student coach. It wasn't what he had planned, but it kept him close to the game he loved. What started as a way to stay connected turned into a calling. That injury? It wasn't just a roadblock — it was the beginning of his journey toward becoming a college and high school coach. It reminds me of Joseph in the Bible. Betrayed by his brothers, sold into slavery, and thrown into prison — his story looked like failure after failure. But through it all, God positioned him to lead and save an entire nation.

Here's the truth: **sometimes God breaks us to break through.** He takes the hard seasons and the painful moments and uses them to reach our hearts in ways we never saw coming. When life throws the unexpected at you, you have a choice—let it break you down or build you into something greater.

God is always working, even when we don't see it. He calls us to trust Him, even when the path looks uncertain. And in the end, He takes our struggles and turns them into something that brings Him glory.

Reflection Questions

1. How have you experienced personal growth during a challenging or painful time in your life?

2. How did that experience deepen your faith or trust in God's plan?

— Coach Diso

71

Ready or Not

"My grace is sufficient for you, for my power is made perfect in weakness." — 2 Corinthians 12:9

No matter how much we prepare, some moments in life still make us feel like we're not ready. The first game of the season, stepping up to the free-throw line with the game on the line, or getting called into the starting lineup for the first time—there's always that voice whispering, *Are you sure you can do this?*

I remember a game where one of our younger players was suddenly thrust into a leadership role. Our starting point guard had fouled out, and this sophomore, who had barely seen the court, had to take control. He looked at me, wide-eyed, as if to say, *Coach, I'm not ready for this.* But I knew better. He had put in the work, studied the plays, and had the heart of a competitor. I told him, *You're as ready as you'll ever be—now go prove it.* And the best part? His teammates rallied around him. They encouraged him, gave him space to lead, and picked him up when he made mistakes. That's what a team does—they carry each other through the fear.

That's often how God works with us. He calls us into situations where we feel unprepared—not because He wants us to fail, but because He wants us to lean on Him. **Failure, by design, is part of the learning process.** We'd never grow if we only stepped into things we felt 100% ready for. **We wouldn't learn how to improve, how to prepare better next time, or how to trust Him more deeply.** We'd never experience the depth of His strength in our weakness. Every missed shot, every stumble, and every tough moment isn't just an obstacle—it's a step forward in becoming who He's shaping us to be.

When you feel unprepared, remind yourself that God isn't asking you to be perfect—He's asking you to be faithful. Perfection was never the requirement—dependence was. He wants your heart, your effort, and your trust. His power shines brightest through our cracks. When you show up with open hands and a willing spirit, He takes care of the rest. His grace is enough, even when you don't feel like you are.

Reflection Question

What's something in your life right now that makes you feel unprepared? How can you trust God's strength instead of your own?

— Coach Dickinson

72

Don't Be Afraid

"And without faith it is impossible to please God, because anyone who comes to him must believe that he exists and that he rewards those who earnestly seek him." — Hebrews 11:6

F aith isn't just a part of our relationship with God—it's the foundation. It's how we come to know Him, trust Him, and follow where He leads. Just like an athlete trains mind and body for competition, we must train our faith. It takes discipline, commitment, and a willingness to push past our doubts.

I saw this play out firsthand, coaching weightlifting. One of my lifters, Sean, found himself ten pounds behind the leader at the state tournament. He had one lift left—a weight he had never attempted in competition. A fifteen-pound jump was a massive challenge for anyone. Before he stepped up to the bar, I pulled him aside. I told him, *If you believe you can do this, you have a shot. But if you doubt yourself for even a second, that weight will crush you. Trust me when I say—you are stronger than you realize.*

At that moment, Sean had a choice. He could give in to fear, or he could trust—trust in his training, his ability, and the truth I was telling him. He stepped onto the platform, took a deep breath, and embraced the moment. That day, he became a state champion.

In that moment, Sean had a choice. He could give in to fear, or he could trust—trust in his training, trust in his ability, and trust in the truth I was speaking over him. More than that, he could trust in the presence of God, who says, *"Fear not, for I am with you... I will strengthen you, I will help you."* Sean stepped onto the platform, took a deep breath, and embraced the moment. That day, he became a state champion—not just because of his strength, but because he chose to trust the One who upholds us with His righteous right hand.

Our faith in God works the same way. **Fear** is one of the biggest roadblocks to faith. It twists our perception and makes us believe we have to rely on our own strength. When we let fear take over, we forget that **God is right there with us**. But Scripture reminds us: *"There is no fear in love. But perfect love drives out fear..."* (1 John 4:18). When we surrender our fears to Him, we step into the unknown with **confidence**, knowing we're not walking alone.

Reflection Questions

1. Where in your life are you struggling to trust God?

2. How can you apply the same mindset of belief and confidence in God's strength to your challenges today?

— Coach Diso

73

Who Do You Say I Am?

"Then He said to them, 'But who do you say that I am?' Peter answered and said, 'The Christ of God.'"
— Luke 9:20 (NKJV)

It's easy to go along with what the crowd says. As an athlete, you hear a lot of opinions—about your performance, your team, your coach, and even yourself. Sometimes, people will label you based on one bad game or a single mistake. Other times, they'll call you a star after one great moment. But who are you, really? And more importantly, who do you say Jesus is?

When we choose to hide rather than face the difficulty, we miss out on the growth that comes from pushing our limits. Just as Coach King stood there—stopwatch in hand, ready to measure our effort—God stands with us in every moment of our lives, guiding and nurturing us through our struggles. His presence isn't just passive observation; it's active engagement in our journey. He's not watching from a distance—He's in it with us. Encouraging. Correcting. Strengthening. Every hardship becomes an opportunity for transformation, not because it's easy, but because He's present.

Take Jonah, for example. He boarded a ship headed in the opposite direction, trying to hide from God's calling. But even in the depths of the sea, God pursued him. Not to punish, but to redeem. Jonah's detour became a defining moment for him. Like Jonah, we may try to avoid what feels too hard, but God doesn't give up on us. He meets us in the storm, the struggle, and even our hiding. Why? Because He's more interested in our growth than our comfort, He knows who we're becoming on the other side of obedience.

As an athlete, you know what it's like to be labeled. Maybe your coach calls you a leader, or maybe you've been told you're not good enough. But at the end of the day, those labels don't define you—Jesus does. And here's the good news: Jesus not only asks who we say He is, but He also tells us who we are in Him.

• **He calls us His beloved** (Romans 9:25).

• **He calls us chosen** (1 Peter 2:9).

• **He calls us His masterpiece** (Ephesians 2:10).

• **He calls us redeemed** (Ephesians 1:7).

Your identity isn't found in what people say about you—it's found in who Christ says you are. And your faith isn't just about what others think of Jesus. It's about who you say He is. Do you just know about Him, or do you truly know Him? Is He just a good teacher in your mind, or is He the Lord of your life?

When the pressure is on, and people ask what you believe, will you confidently declare, "Jesus is my Savior, and in Him, I am chosen, loved, and redeemed"?

Reflection Question

If Jesus were to ask you today, "Who do you say that I am?"—and if He answered back, "And here's who I say you are"—would you believe Him over what the world says about you?

Final Challenge

Take a moment today to write down who Jesus says you are. Do you believe it? Are you living like it?

— Coach Dickinson

74

God is the Path

The Lord is good and does what is right. He shows the proper path to those who go astray. He leads the humble in doing right, teaching them his way. The Lord leads with unfailing love and faithfulness all who keep his covenant and obey his commands — Psalm 25:8-10

Every team—whether in sports, work, or life—has that one teammate who sets the tone. The one who shows up early puts in the work and encourages everyone else to rise to the challenge. Their dedication isn't just about personal success; it lifts the entire team. Their effort in the classroom, on the field, and in relationships is consistent. When things get tough, they don't back down. They speak life into others, bring the energy, and make sure no one gets left behind. That kind of teammate is priceless.

Our spiritual journey works the same way. There's a difference between knowing about God and actually trusting Him. It's easy to say, "God is good," when life is smooth. But what about when it isn't? That's when real faith is revealed. Do we believe in His goodness even when things fall apart? Do we trust His plan even when it doesn't make sense? The truth is, we don't always get to define what *"good"* looks like. But we can trust that God is always good. To us, good often means comfort, ease, or success. But to God, good looks like growth, refinement, and becoming more like Christ.

Romans 8:28–29 reminds us that God works all things together for good *"for those who love Him"*—and that good is that we are *"conformed to the image of His Son."* But we can trust that God is always good. That's why the phrase, *"God is good all the time, and all the time, God is good,"* isn't just something we say—it's something we're called to live.

When life gets messy, it's easy to get stuck in our heads, focusing on everything going wrong. But shifting our focus—choosing praise over worry, gratitude over frustration—changes everything. Lifting our eyes to God reminds us that we're never alone. Like a great teammate strengthens a team, finding a community of believers to help our connection with God strengthens our lives. His love, guidance, and purpose carry us through every challenge, shaping us into who we were meant to be.

Reflection Questions

1. How does the way a committed teammate impacts a team reflect how God moves in our lives?

2. When you're struggling, how can shifting your focus to gratitude and worship help deepen your trust in God?

— Coach Diso

75

Built by Fire

"The crucible for silver and the furnace for gold, but the Lord tests the heart." – Proverbs 17:3

"Consider it pure joy, my brothers and sisters, whenever you face trials of many kinds, because you know that the testing of your faith produces perseverance. Let perseverance finish its work so that you may be mature and complete, not lacking anything." – James 1:2-4

"These [trials] have come so that the proven genuineness of your faith—of greater worth than gold, which perishes even though refined by fire—may result in praise, glory, and honor when Jesus Christ is revealed." – 1 Peter 1:6-7

You don't know what you're made of until the fire tests you.

It's one thing to show up for summer workouts. It's another thing to endure them. Every year, I watched the linemen struggle through those first few days of two-a-days. These weren't guys built for speed—they were built for war. Carrying an extra 100+ pounds, they faced a different kind of challenge.

Every sprint felt like dragging a cinder block uphill. Every drill left them gasping. Every step tested their will. Some of them wanted to quit. Some probably should have quit. But those who stayed? Those who pushed through? They didn't just survive. **They transformed.**

By the time the season kicked off, the same guys who had been bent over in exhaustion became the foundation of our team's success. They weren't just big anymore. They were built for battle.

The same is true in our walk with Christ.

God never wastes the fire. The trials you're facing aren't meant to break you—they're meant to build something deeper in you: perseverance, humility, trust. James tells us to "consider it pure joy" when facing struggles because those struggles develop spiritual endurance. Peter reminds us that our faith is like gold—it's being refined to remove impurities, leaving behind something stronger and purer. Proverbs clarifies that God tests our hearts to strengthen our character and align it with His.

The question is: **Will you endure?**

The linemen who pushed through those brutal weeks didn't immediately see the results. They questioned if it was worth it. But they kept showing up—and they didn't do it alone. They leaned on each other. They encouraged the guy beside them, picked each other up, and found strength in the shared struggle. By the time the season started, their transformation was undeniable. The fire had worked—not just on the individual but on the brotherhood.

Maybe you're in that fire right now. Maybe you're gasping for air, wondering if you can keep going. Maybe the weight feels too heavy.

Keep going.

God is refining you. This fire has a purpose. And if you endure, you won't just survive. You'll be built for battle.

Reflection Question

What "fire" are you walking through right now, and how is God using it to refine you?

— Coach Dickinson

76

TWT

"The Lord is near to all who call on him, to all who call on him in truth." — Psalms 145:19

As I reminisce about those grueling Monday track practices in high school, I can almost feel the scorching Florida sun beating down on us as we lined up to run. Mondays were our "quarters" day—the most challenging practice of the week. Coach King would often scream, "TWT!" at us during practice. He would shout with a fierceness that could cut through a steak. It meant "Time Will Tell," but it felt like a burden at the time. Back then, I couldn't see the profound truth embedded in those three simple words.

When we choose to hide rather than face the difficulty, we miss out on the growth that comes from pushing our limits. Just as Coach King stood there—stopwatch in hand, ready to measure our effort—God stands with us in every moment of our lives, guiding and nurturing us through our struggles. His presence isn't just passive observation; it's active engagement in our journey. He's not watching from a distance—He's in it with us. Encouraging. Correcting. Strengthening. Every hardship becomes an opportunity for transformation, not because it's easy, but because He's present.

Take Jonah, for example. He boarded a ship headed in the opposite direction, trying to hide from God's calling. But even in the depths of the sea, God pursued him. Not to punish, but to redeem. Jonah's detour became a defining moment for him. Just like Jonah, we may try to avoid what feels too hard, but God doesn't give up on us. He meets us in the storm, in the struggle, and even in our hiding. Why? Because He's more interested in our growth than our comfort—and He knows who we're becoming on the other side of obedience.

Much like the laps we ran, life can often feel repetitive and exhausting. There are days we wish we could escape—days when hiding in a restroom stall seems like the easier option than running on the track (and yes, players were guilty of this). Yet God uses those very circumstances—the heat of the moment, the fatigue in our bones—to mold us into something stronger. He invites us to embrace the discomfort, reminding us that growth often comes from the trials we face.

In moments when we feel abandoned or alone, we must remember that God is always present and at work, crafting our character and shaping our destinies, even when we cannot see His hands moving. It's in the quiet moments of reflection, the pauses between our breaths, that we can truly hear Him whispering encouragement into our souls.

So, as we lace up our sneakers for the day ahead, let's approach each challenge with the mindset that TWT isn't just about time revealing the outcome—it's about faithfully trusting that God is never absent and is working, even in the unseen. Let's stay awake to His presence, open our hearts to His guidance, and allow our circumstances to transform us into vessels of His purpose. After all, the greatest victories come not from avoiding the race but from running it with faith, determination, and an unfaltering belief that we are never alone.

Reflection Questions

1. How can the phrase TWT (Time Will Tell) serve as a reminder to trust in God's timing and presence, especially during moments of difficulty and uncertainty?

2. In what ways can we embrace discomfort and challenges, knowing that they are opportunities for growth and transformation?

— Coach Diso

77

The Nature of Things

"For since the creation of the world God's invisible qualities—his eternal power and divine nature—have been clearly seen, being understood from what has been made, so that people are without excuse." — Romans 1:20 (NIV)

Everything in creation has a nature—a purpose and design that align with God's perfect order. Trees reach for sunlight, absorb water, and grow deep roots. Birds instinctively migrate, build nests, and care for their young. Even a two-year-old behaves exactly like a two-year-old should, with boundless energy, curiosity, and a streak of defiance that reminds us they are learning their limits.

Athletes understand this concept well. A sprinter is designed to explode out of the blocks with speed, while a marathon runner is built for endurance. A basketball player must refine their footwork and precision, while a football lineman must develop strength and resilience. Each athlete thrives when they train and perform according to their natural strengths, but when they attempt to play outside of their design—forcing speed when built for endurance or vice versa—they struggle. Ignoring their design leads to failure, fatigue, and even injury.

God designed every part of creation with precision. A tree does not decide one day to live underwater, just as a bird does not abandon its wings and choose to crawl. Each thing in creation follows the order it was designed for, and in that design, it thrives.

Humans, however, are unique. God gave us free will—the ability to choose how we live. Unlike trees, birds, or animals, we can reject the nature God has given us. We can step outside of His design for how we should live, how we should love, and how we should worship. But while we have the freedom to make those choices, we do not have the power to escape the consequences. Just as a fish cannot survive out of water, we cannot flourish when we step outside of God's order.

Throughout history, humanity has been tempted to redefine what God has made, often exchanging truth for confusion. The enemy wants us to believe that we can redefine what God has already perfected. Just as an athlete thrives when training within their natural abilities, we find true peace and fulfillment when we align with the purpose God has given us. Our identity is not something we construct but something we receive as a gift from God, woven into the very fabric of our being. Our nature is not something we choose; it is a gift from God, designed with purpose and intention.

God's design is not flawed. It does not need human adjustment, improvement, or reinvention. Just as God's design for individuals is intentional, so too is His design for marriage. Marriage also has a nature, designed by God to be a lifelong covenant between a man and a woman. When this design is broken through divorce, the consequences ripple through generations—children growing up in broken homes, the loss of stability, and deep emotional wounds.

God's intention for marriage is not just for companionship but for the flourishing of families and society as a whole. The world tries to redefine roles, identities, and purpose, but God's blueprint has never changed. He created fathers with a nature. He created mothers with a nature. He created each of us to need food, clothing, shelter—and, most importantly, love and belonging. When we live as He intended, we experience peace and fulfillment. When we reject that design, we struggle, facing the consequences of a life outside of His will.

The good news is that no matter how far we stray from our intended nature, God always welcomes us back. His grace is big enough to restore what we have broken. The choice is ours: live according to His perfect design or suffer the consequences of ignoring it. We may attempt to shape reality according to our desires, but reality itself is rooted in God's eternal truth. When we embrace His design, we experience the wholeness and harmony He intended.

Reflection Question

In what ways am I living outside of the nature God designed for me? How can I realign my life with His perfect plan, and what practical steps can I take today to embrace His design?

— Coach Dickinson

78

God is Power

"And he became more and more powerful, because the Lord God Almighty was with him." — 2 Samuel 5:10

Strength training is a game-changer. Athletes who put in the work—hitting the weight room, pushing through sprints, grinding out reps—see the results. Speed. Power. Confidence. There's no denying that getting stronger gives you an edge in competition. But here's the truth: no amount of physical strength can prepare you for life's toughest battles. Eventually, you'll hit a challenge that no amount of muscle can move.

But God? He never hits a limit. He is all-powerful. No opponent can stand against Him; no force can stop Him. With a single word, He created the universe. With another, He could tear it down. He doesn't need anyone or anything—He simply *is* strength. His power isn't just massive—it's unmatched, infinite, and unshakable.

That's the kind of strength I depend on. It's not the weight I lift or the speed I gain—it's *His* power that carries me. When I face adversity, when life throws me to the mat, when I feel like I can't take another step, *He* is my endurance. He provides, He protects, and He strengthens me in ways no training program ever could.

Here's the best part: God doesn't just flex His power from a distance—He gives it to us. When He calls us to something, He equips us to handle it. No challenge is too big when He's in our corner. That's why I don't rely on my own strength—I trust in His. Spiritual disciplines like prayer, Scripture, and worship aren't about earning God's favor—they're about training our hearts to depend on His strength instead of our own. They create space for us to slow down, listen, and remember who the power really belongs to. *"He gives strength to the weary and increases the power of the weak."* (Isaiah 40:29)

The weight room might build my body, but God's power strengthens my soul. And in the biggest moments—the ones that actually matter—I know where my strength comes from.

Reflection Questions

1. How can you rely on God's strength in your daily life?

2. In what ways can you use the confidence gained from physical training to deepen your trust in God's power and depend on Him more fully?

— Coach Diso

79

Trust the Playbook

"Trust in the Lord with all your heart and lean not on your own understanding; in all your ways submit to him, and he will make your paths straight."
— Proverbs 3:5-6 (NIV)

Every great team has a playbook—a set of plays designed for victory. A coach doesn't put together a game plan randomly; he studies the opponent, assesses his team's strengths, and creates a strategy that will lead to success. Now, imagine a rookie quarterback who refuses to follow the playbook. He decides he knows better, ignores the game plan, and does his own thing. What happens? He fails. Every time. Not because he lacks talent, but because he didn't trust the system that was designed to help him win.

The Bible is God's playbook for our lives. It's been tested, proven, and remains undefeated. Yet, just like that rookie QB, we sometimes think we know better. We hesitate, we doubt, or we believe the world's ever-changing philosophies over God's unchanging truth. But here's the reality: God's Word isn't just a set of suggestions—it's the blueprint for life. And it stands firm on solid evidence.

How Do We Know the Bible is True?

The Bible Has Been Preserved with Unmatched Accuracy

- The Dead Sea Scrolls (discovered in 1947) show that the Scriptures we have today are nearly identical to manuscripts from over 2,000 years ago. God has protected His Word through time.

It's Historically Reliable

- Archaeology continues to confirm people, places, and events recorded in the Bible. For example, historians once thought the Hittites were a fictional people—until archaeological evidence proved they were real, just as the Bible said.

Eyewitness Accounts

- The New Testament isn't based on legends passed down over centuries—it was written by people who witnessed Jesus' miracles, death, and resurrection firsthand. These were the very people who went from hiding in fear to boldly preaching Christ, many of them dying for what they saw.

Prophecies Fulfilled (No Other Book Does This)

- Over 300 prophecies about Jesus—written centuries before He was born—came true. Example: Isaiah 53 describes His crucifixion in detail—700 years before it happened. No human could predict that without divine inspiration.

Changed Lives

- The Bible has transformed millions of lives throughout history. The disciples went from fearful and hiding to boldly preaching and dying for their faith. Today, people from every nation and background still find purpose, healing, and salvation through its truth.

Trusting the Playbook

Imagine a quarterback stepping onto the field without studying the playbook. Disaster. Now, imagine a quarterback who memorizes the plays, trusts the system, and executes the plan with confidence. That's how championships are won.

The Bible is our playbook for life. The more we study it, trust it, and apply it, the more we walk in victory. God's Word is not outdated, irrelevant, or untrustworthy—it is living, active, and undefeated. The real question is: will you trust the playbook or try to run your own plays?

Reflection Questions

1. Have I fully trusted the Bible as God's true and proven playbook for my life?

2. What step can I take today to study and apply God's Word more faithfully?

— Coach Dickinson

80

Mind Games

"But letting the Spirit control your mind leads to life and peace" — Romans 8:6

U ncomfortable moments in sports competitions are part of the journey, shaping not just athletes but the very essence of competition itself. I vividly recall a moment involving a prominent wrestler on our team named Jason. The pressure was monumental; he was being hailed as a potential state champion. However, when his mother came to watch him compete for the first time ever, something unexpected unfolded. On that fateful day, the excitement of having her in the stands for the first time coupled with the intense desire to perform at his best became a double-edged sword.

Despite his training and supreme skills, Jason lost that match by a narrow point. It was an astonishing twist of fate that left him disheartened. Though he went on to finish third that season—a commendable achievement that capped off his record-setting career—one can't help but wonder how it felt to bear the burden of that unexpected defeat. In hindsight, while Jason would have loved to rewrite that chapter, it reminds us that God prioritizes our transformation over altering our circumstances. We often pray for our problems, fears, and pain to vanish, yet God is more invested in working on "us." True transformation begins in the mind; it requires a renewing of our thoughts and attitudes.

Our thoughts have immense power—they shape our perceptions and even our reality. When we harbor negative self-perceptions, those thoughts often spill over into our interactions and influence others negatively. Thus, the mind becomes a battleground where we must consciously choose to let God govern our thoughts. Like Jason, whose mind was filled with pressures, finding peace and joy starts within. A healthy mindset fosters confidence and hope, equipping us to handle stress, fear, and frustration more effectively.

This journey toward mental wellness isn't passive—it demands effort --we must feed our minds with truth. In a world riddled with lies and negativity, anchoring ourselves in God's word is crucial. His truth realigns our thoughts, renews our perspective, and reminds us of who we are in Him. *"Do not conform to the pattern of this world, but be transformed by the renewing of your mind. Then you will be able to test and approve what God's will is—His good, pleasing, and perfect will."* (Romans 12:2)

Daily meditation on His truths replenishes our spirits and strengthens our minds against the adversities life presents. By focusing on what pleases God, we align ourselves with the blessings He desires for us. It's through this daily engagement with scripture that we positive mental environment—one where God is at the forefront, guiding our thoughts and actions. Let's strive to live lives filled with God's presence in our hearts and minds. By taking our thoughts captive and weaving prayer into our daily routine, we make God the focal point of our reflections. Embracing this approach not only empowers us to overcome personal setbacks—like the one Jason faced on a wrestling mat —but also unlocks the joy and peace that come from knowing we are continuously transformed through His love.

Reflection Questions

1. How can you reshape your mindset to view uncomfortable moments or setbacks as opportunities for personal and spiritual growth?

2. In what ways can you actively work on renewing your thoughts and aligning them with God's truths?

— Coach Diso

81

Trust And.

"Blessed is the one who trusts in the Lord, whose confidence is in him. They will be like a tree planted by the water that sends out its roots by the stream. It does not fear when heat comes; its leaves are always green. It has no worries in a year of drought and never fails to bear fruit." — Jeremiah 17:7-8

"Trust in the Lord with all your heart and lean not on your own understanding; in all your ways submit to him, and he will make your paths straight." — Proverbs 3:5-6

There's a difference between saying you trust and actually trusting. You see it all the time in sports. A player says, "I trust my coach, but I don't like this game plan." Or, "I trust my training, but I don't know if I can perform under pressure." That's not trust—it's doubt dressed up in safe words.

Real trust doesn't come with a backup plan. It's not halfway in. It's all-in.

A lot of people do the same thing with God. They say:

- "I trust God, but I need to have everything figured out first."

- "I trust God, but I don't want to step out of my comfort zone."

- "I trust God, but what if I fail?"

That little "but" is where fear lives. It's where hesitation and control creep in. It's where we say we trust while still keeping one hand on the wheel.

Jeremiah 17:7-8 describes trust like a tree planted by the water. A tree doesn't sit there questioning whether the water is enough. It doesn't say, "I trust the water, but what if there's a drought?" It just trusts. Its roots go deep. It soaks up what it's given and stands strong, no matter what's happening around it.

Athletes who trust their training don't hesitate when the game is on the line. They don't say, "I trust my shot, but maybe I should pass." They say, "I trust my shot, and I'm taking it."

Peter had a choice when Jesus called him out onto the water (Matthew 14:28-31). If he had said, "I trust You, but I'm afraid of sinking," he never would have stepped out of the boat. Instead, he trusted and moved. It was only when doubt crept in that he started to sink.

So what does "Trust And." look like?

- "I trust God, and I will take the next step even when I don't see the whole path."

- "I trust God, and I know He is in control, even when life feels uncertain."

- "I trust God, and I will keep going, knowing He is with me in victory and in failure."

Trust isn't about feeling safe. It's about surrender. No excuses. No hesitation. **Trust.**

Reflection Question

This week, catch yourself when you're about to say, "Trust but." Replace it with "Trust And.," and see how it changes your mindset. What's one area of your life where you need to go all-in on trust?

— Coach Dickinson

82

What are You Choosing?

"And that you may love the Lord your God, listen to his voice, and hold fast to him. For the Lord is your life, and he will give you many years..." — Deuteronomy 30:20

In the life of an athlete, the path is often laden with challenges that test not just physical strength but mental resolve. Decisions loom large, and quitting can seem like the easiest route when faced with adversity. Many athletes, including myself, have grappled with the notion of walking away—an instinctive response to disappointment and defeat. However, it is in these moments of doubt that true character is forged.

Take Ricky, for example. His junior year, he faced a critical choice after being cut during baseball tryouts. The sting of rejection weighed heavily as he contemplated walking away from sports entirely. Friends encouraged him to quit, suggesting it was time to move on. But I saw something in Ricky that he couldn't yet see in himself—a potential waiting to be unleashed. I invited him to try out for a new sport, emphasizing that his athleticism could still shine on a different field.

The decision to give it a shot instead of walking away was monumental. Ricky chose to embrace the challenge, stepping out of his comfort zone and into an arena that would ultimately redefine his athletic journey. His hard work and determination, he didn't just find success on the team—he opened the door to opportunities that extended far beyond high school athletics. By choosing perseverance over resignation, Ricky unlocked a future aligned with his passions and talents.

His story echoes the perseverance of the Apostle Paul, who faced beatings, shipwrecks, imprisonment, and rejection yet remained faithful to his calling. Paul didn't let setbacks define him; instead, he pressed on with confidence in God's purpose. *"I press on toward the goal to win the prize for which God has called me heavenward in Christ Jesus."*(Philippians 3:14) Like Paul, Ricky's decision to persevere through difficulty became a turning point—not just for personal success, but for a deeper alignment with his purpose.

This experience echoes the timeless wisdom found in Deuteronomy, where we are reminded that our choices carry significant weight. As athletes—and as individuals—we are presented with crossroads that demand courage and faith. Each decision is not merely a reflection of our immediate desires but shapes our integrity, character, and habits. Upholding values that mirror our faith is crucial; it is a testament to a life lived in obedience to God's purpose.

The joy and peace that come from following God's path far surpass short-lived moments of discomfort. Choosing to persevere through trials fosters resilience and deepens our connection with our faith. It not only transforms our individual journeys but also impacts those around us.

In moments of doubt, let us remember those who have chosen to push forward, embracing new challenges rather than retreating. Let us walk this path with Jesus, reflecting His light through our choices and inspiring others to do the same. Ultimately, the greatest victories are often born from moments when we choose to keep fighting, even when the odds seem stacked against us.

Reflection Questions

1. Describe a moment when you had to persevere through rejection or make a hard choice.

2. In what ways do the choices we make in times of doubt shape our character and align us with God's purpose? How can we lean on our faith to guide us through life's crossroads?

— Coach Diso

83

The Road Less Chosen

"Enter through the narrow gate. For wide is the gate and broad is the road that leads to destruction, and many enter through it. But small is the gate and narrow the road that leads to life, and only a few find it." — Matthew 7:13-14 (NIV)

There's always an easier way. The road that requires less effort, less sacrifice, and, quite frankly, less resistance. It's the road where everyone else seems to be walking—where compromise is common, shortcuts are normal, and excuses are accepted. Spiritually, it might look like skipping time in the Word, serving only when convenient, or only praying when there's a crisis. It's tempting because, at first glance, it looks like the best choice. But as Matthew 7:13–14 reminds us, that road doesn't lead to life.

I remember watching players run sprints around the football field. The instructions were clear: go to the corner, touch the line, and keep running. Most of them did. But occasionally, someone would cut the corner just enough to save a little time and effort. The coaches weren't always watching, but I noticed. And when it came time for that player to show up in the fourth quarter, in the heat of the battle, when every ounce of discipline mattered—they were the ones who ran out of gas first.

The same thing happens in life. You can be the athlete who skips reps, takes the easy way, and rounds the corners just enough so no one notices. That's the wide road. Plenty of people take it. But it always catches up to them in the end.

Then there's the narrow road. The one where you do what's right even when no one is watching. Where you go all the way to the line because you know that discipline built in the dark—the moments of obedience no one sees, the quiet sacrifices, the integrity behind closed doors—will show up in the light. It shows up in your witness, your strength when life tests you, and the trust others place in your character. Jesus never promised that following Him would be easy. He made it clear that most people wouldn't choose the narrow road. But He did promise that the narrow road leads to life. True life. Eternal life. And in the end, that's the only road worth traveling.

Reflection Question

Are you rounding the corners in your faith, character, and discipline, or are you running all the way to the line?

— Coach Dickinson

84

Worry or Prayer?

"Be anxious for nothing, but in everything by prayer and supplication with thanksgiving let your requests be made known to God." — Philippians 4:6

Ryan had always dreamed of wearing the orange and blue of the Florida Gators. He put in countless hours of practice, set records, and earned accolades as one of the top high school players in the nation at his position. Yet, despite his achievements, the coveted offer from UF never materialized.

The disappointment weighed heavily on him. I remember the countless nights we spent discussing his dreams and his anxiety over not receiving that elusive scholarship. He desperately wanted to prove himself that I took him to a showcase camp at the University of Florida, where he shined brighter than anyone else on the field. He was electric, dominating every drill. And yet, still, no offer came.

In the aftermath—when hope seemed just out of reach—we talked deeply about the nature of worry. I reminded him that anxiety is a thief of joy and productivity, echoing the wisdom found in Philippians. "God is my help and refuge," I said, instilling a sense of peace in his heart. I encouraged him to embrace the truth that no detail of his life went unnoticed by God and that divine eyes were upon him even in his darkest moments. Eventually, after committing to another college and having a stellar senior season, the Gators finally came knocking. It was bittersweet. The dream he had held close for so long and the journey that had tested his resolve all came rushing back. Yet, through it all, I was reminded of our conversations—how peace is possible even in uncertainty.

I reflected on how worry had never produced fruit — only weighed us down with burdens too heavy to carry. I shared with Ryan that casting all our fears and anxieties toward heaven brings freedom. As Scripture reminds us, *"Cast all your anxiety on Him because He cares for you."* (1 Peter 5:7). *"He is my provider when I need help,"* I told him, remembering those anxious days we faced together. *"He comforts me when I need calming, and He gives me strength when I am weary."*

The moment Ryan received that offer was not just the realization of a long-held dream — it was a testament to resilience and faith. It was a celebration of the journey — the struggles along the way and the understanding that true peace really does transcend understanding. His journey wasn't easy, but he stayed rooted, trusting that God was working, even in the silence. As he stepped onto the field, donning the Gators' colors, he carried with him his talent and a heart fortified by faith and the understanding that sometimes, waiting leads to the most beautiful blessings.

Reflection Questions

1. What is one thing you are working hard for that you haven't received?

2. In what ways can casting our anxieties and fears toward God help us navigate uncertainty and bring peace?

— Coach Diso

85

Soaring Through The Storm

"But those who wait on the Lord shall renew their strength; They shall mount up with wings like eagles, They shall run and not be weary, They shall walk and not faint." — Isaiah 40:31

Athletes know the grind. You push yourself to the limit—lungs burning, legs screaming, every ounce of energy drained. There are moments in a game, a practice, or a season when you don't know if you can keep going. But somehow, you do. Somehow, strength comes when you think you have nothing left. That kind of strength doesn't just come from muscle—it comes from mental discipline and spiritual trust. *Waiting on the Lord* for an athlete might look like praying before a big moment, staying consistent in your Bible reading during the off-season, or choosing rest when the world says, "Go harder." It's not passive—it's faithful preparation.

That's what Isaiah 40:31 is all about. God doesn't promise we'll never get tired, face adversity, or feel weak. But He does promise that if we wait on Him and trust Him, He will renew our strength. He will lift us like eagles, giving us what we need exactly when we need it.

Isaiah 40 was written to the people of Israel during a time of deep discouragement. They were in exile, beaten down, and wondering if God had abandoned them. Through Isaiah, God reminded them of who He is—the Creator of the universe, the One who never grows tired, the One who holds power over all nations.

Just before this verse, Isaiah 40:28 asks, "Do you not know? Have you not heard? The Lord is the everlasting God, the Creator of the ends of the earth. He will not grow tired or weary, and His understanding no one can fathom." In other words, God is never exhausted, overwhelmed, or out of control. And when we trust in Him, He shares His strength with us.

A lot of times, you don't see the good God is doing until you look back. I've lived this. There was a time in my life when I was in a storm so heavy I couldn't see a way through. I didn't understand why God allowed it or what He was doing. It felt like I was running with no finish line in sight, just trying to survive. But now, looking back, I see His hand in every part of it. He was strengthening me, shaping me, and teaching me to trust.

This verse reminds me that I don't need to wait until I look back to trust Him in my next storm. I can trust Him in the middle of it. Just like an eagle doesn't fight against the wind but soars on it, we don't have to fight our struggles alone—we can rise above them by leaning into God's strength. Eagles are built to rise higher when storms come—their wings are designed to catch the wind and climb. In the same way, when we stop striving for our own strength and rely on God's power, we find a new level of endurance and peace. Athletes who learn to soar this way don't burn out—they rise.

So when you feel exhausted, overwhelmed, or unsure of what's next, remember Isaiah 40:31. Keep running. Keep trusting. God is renewing your strength, even if you can't see it yet.

Reflection Question

Think of a time when you couldn't see God's purpose in a tough situation but later realized He was working through it. How can you remind yourself to trust Him in the middle of the storm, not just after it?

— Coach Dickinson

86

Good All the Time?

"For the Lord is good and his love endures forever." – Psalm 100:5

Let's be real—it's easy to question everything when life hits hard. Injuries. Coaching changes. Broken plans. You start wondering if all the dreams you were chasing are even possible.

That's precisely where Wadzaire found himself.

The guy was on fire. Full-ride offers. All-American honors. His future was lined up like a highlight reel waiting to happen. Then—boom. In one moment, it all came crashing down. A freak injury caused nerve damage that left his right arm paralyzed. Just like that, the lights dimmed, and everything felt uncertain. Coaches stopped calling. People started doubting.

But God? He never left.

We had to remind Wadzaire of something powerful: *God's love doesn't depend on your stats, your scholarship offers, or your circumstances.* His love *endures*—through pain, through setbacks, through silence. That's the anchor that kept Wadzaire from sinking.

After a year of rehab and heartbreak, a miracle showed up. Emergency surgery gave him a shot at healing. He didn't waste it. He grinded in silence. He fought to get back. And when senior year rolled around, he did the unthinkable—suited up for the season's final game. First game back in two years. And what does he do? Scores the first playoff touchdown in school history.

That's not luck. That's purpose.

Wadzaire's comeback wasn't just about football. It was about **faith that refuses to quit**, even when everything falls apart. It was about trusting that God is good *even when life feels bad*. That's not easy. But it's real. And it's powerful.

Here's the deal: God isn't just good when things are good. He's good *all the time*. Even in the setbacks. Even in the silence. Even in the waiting rooms and the "Why me?" moments.

Wadzaire's story is proof that your worst days don't get the final say. God does. And His plan? It's bigger than you can imagine. In his lowest moments, the community lifted him up—teammates who showed up, coaches who believed in him, friends and family who reminded him of who he was when he started to forget. Their prayers, encouragement, and presence became the steady hands that helped carry him through.

So, whatever you're facing — don't give up. Let your faith carry you through. And when that comeback moment arrives, you'll realize it wasn't just about you. It was about every person watching. Every teammate who needed hope. Every future athlete who will hear your story and believe that with God, anything is possible.

Reflection Questions

1. When life hits hard, how can you lean into your faith and let it carry you through uncertainty?

2. How can your setbacks become someone else's inspiration? What story is God writing through your struggle?

— Coach Diso

87

Running The Race With Micah 6:8

"He has shown you, O mortal, what is good. And what does the Lord require of you? To act justly and to love mercy and to walk humbly with your God." — Micah 6:8

Athletes, you know what it means to push hard—sprinting toward the finish line, grinding through practice, or squeezing out one more rep when your body is begging you to quit. But here's a question: *What's driving you?* Micah 6:8 lays out a different kind of game plan—the one that matters beyond the scoreboard.

Micah was a prophet speaking to people who had lost their way. They were cheating each other, chasing power, and forgetting God. Sound familiar? In a world obsessed with winning at all costs, Micah cuts through the noise. God isn't looking for flashy sacrifices or empty rituals. He wants three things: justice, mercy, and humility.

On the field, acting justly might mean playing fair even when the ref isn't looking—honoring the game and your teammates. As a team, it means standing up for what's right, even when it's uncomfortable. Loving mercy could look like encouraging a teammate who's struggling, picking up a rival after a brutal hit, or forgiving someone who let you down—walking humbly with God. That's knowing your strength comes from Him, not just your training—and reminding each other of that truth, even in the middle of competition.

I've seen this play out beyond sports, too. My dad lived this verse. Micah 6:8 wasn't just words to him—it was a way of life. He even wrote a song about it—simple, but it stuck with you. I can still hear him humming, *"Do justly, love mercy, walk humbly with your God."* It wasn't just a song for him—it was how he lived. He treated people right, showed kindness, and stayed grounded. He wasn't an athlete in the stadium sense, but he ran the race the right way.

Micah 6:8 is more than just a moral checklist—it reflects Jesus Himself. Jesus embodied justice by defending the outcast, mercy by forgiving His enemies, and humility by laying down His life. When we live out this verse, we're not just doing good—we're following the example of Christ. That's what makes this calling not just powerful but personal.

This verse meant so much to me that I ended up writing a book about it—*Micah 6:8: A Prophetic Bridge to Jesus*. It explores how this simple but powerful call to justice, mercy, and humility ultimately points to Christ. If this devotion resonates with you, you'll find that book to be a deeper dive into how we can live out God's calling every day.

So, next practice or game, think about Micah 6:8. How can you bring justice, mercy, and humility to your hustle? You might not write a song like my dad did, but you can live it out—one play at a time.

Reflection Questions

1. What's one way you can "act justly" in your sport this week?

2. How can you show mercy to a teammate, opponent, or yourself?

3. What does it look like to walk humbly with God as an athlete?

— Coach Dickinson

88

Remain Selfless

"Do nothing out of selfish ambition or vain conceit. Rather, in humility value others above yourself." – Philippians 2:3

L et me tell you about Shay.

This dude didn't have the spotlight. No hype, no special treatment. He just showed up—day after day—working like crazy while feeling like no one was watching. The coaches had their eyes on other players, and no matter how much effort Shay put in, it seemed like he was invisible.

That kind of thing can eat you up if you let it.

But Shay? He kept grinding. He never let bitterness take root. He still backed his teammates. He respected the decisions—even when they hurt. That's rare. That's character.

Then, something shifted. A new coach showed up, and a fresh set of eyes came with him. Suddenly, all those early mornings, all the reps no one clapped for, started to matter. Shay didn't just get better—he *exploded*. He broke a state record and went from unknown to unforgettable. Everyone knew his name. But here's the real win—he never let it go to his head. He stayed the same humble, hardworking guy who once felt invisible.

Shay's story hits deep because it's not just about football—it's about life.

There will be times when you feel like your effort doesn't matter. Like you're being passed over. Like no one sees how hard you're trying. But hear me loud and clear: **God sees you.** He sees the hustle when no one else does. And He's not just watching—He's *shaping* you.

Waiting isn't wasted time. It's the training ground — for your character, faith, and purpose. Shay's breakthrough didn't happen despite the struggle — it happened because of it. Through the long road of uncertainty, faith was the foundation that helped him stay grounded. When emotions ran high and circumstances felt unfair, he didn't react out of frustration — he responded in faith.

His trust in God helped him maintain his integrity, even when no one was watching. He trusted that even in the silence, God was still working. So stay ready. Stay selfless. Keep serving your teammates. Keep showing respect. Keep choosing grace over gossip. Every act of humility, the choice to love instead of lash out, and quiet sacrifice adds up. Jesus didn't chase glory. He served. And that's what true greatness looks like. So, what kind of legacy are you building? Let your life be more than stats or trophies. Let it be a light. Let it be love.

Reflection Questions

1. When you're stuck waiting or feeling frustrated, how can

you use that time to grow in skill, character, and humility?

2. Think about a time you felt overlooked. How can that experience motivate you to serve others with more faith and purpose?

— Coach Diso

89

The Change is Worth It

"Therefore, if anyone is in Christ, he is a new creation. The old has passed away; behold, the new has come." — 2 Corinthians 5:17

When you commit to following Christ, everything changes. Your old life—how you thought, spoke, and acted—looks different. The Bible says the old self is gone, and the new self has come. That means Christ now lives in you, and from that moment on, a battle begins:
More of Jesus. Less of me.

And that change? It truly changes everything.

Your priorities shift. The way you see the world is different. Relationships with family, friends, and teammates might change. Some people won't understand. You may even lose friends. Some family members might distance themselves.
But here's the truth—you're not losing. **You're gaining.**

- You're gaining a purpose that matters.

- You're gaining an identity not tied to performance, status, or approval.

- You're gaining a Savior who will never walk away, even when others do.

Yes, change is hard. Some days, it will feel like an uphill battle. But the transformation God is working in you? It's worth it—every time.

Reflection Question

Where do you feel the tug-of-war between your old self and your new self in Christ—on the field, with teammates, or in your personal goals? How can you choose more of Jesus there today?

— Coach Dickinson

90

Teammates

"Trust in the Lord with all your heart and lean not on your own understanding." – Proverbs 3:5

Let's talk about slumps. Whether it's on the field, in the weight room, or just in life—you've been there. That moment when nothing's clicking, and you start questioning if you've still got it.

Now imagine being Jesus—the Son of God—and still knowing you needed people around you. That's wild, right? But it's true. Jesus didn't go it alone. He built a team. He called His disciples not just to learn from Him but to walk *with* Him. They weren't perfect. Far from it. But they were His people—His teammates.

And that tells us something important: **we're not meant to do this life alone.**

Your circle matters. Big time.

You need people around you who aren't just about hype but about *heart*. Teammates who care more about your character than your stats. Friends who push you closer to Jesus, not farther away.

Mentors who show up when you're struggling and speak truth when you're confused. That's real community. And it's powerful.

Yes, there's value in solitude—Jesus took time to be alone with the Father. But He always came back to the team. Shared meals. Long walks. Deep talks. That rhythm of prayer *and* people kept Him grounded. It can do the same for you.

So, who's in your huddle?

Are you plugged into a Bible study group, youth ministry, or just a solid group of friends chasing after the same goal—to know Jesus more? If not, find it. Build it. Be it.

Jesus took time to be alone with the Father. But He always came back to the team. Shared meals. Long walks. Deep talks. That rhythm of prayer and people kept Him grounded. And it can do the same for you. If the Son of God needed both time with the Father and time with His people, how much more do we? We were created not just for connection with God but for deep, life-giving connection with others. Community isn't just a bonus—it's essential.

Because when life gets heavy—and it will—your teammates will remind you of who you are and who you are. They'll help you stand when you want to sit, pray when you feel too tired, and speak the truth when the lies get loud. Together, you can face challenges with faith instead of fear. A strong community isn't just a support system—it's a spiritual anchor.

That's why Scripture calls us to live intentionally with others:

"And let us consider how we may spur one another on toward love and good deeds." — **Hebrews 10:24**

This is what real community does. It spurs. It lifts. It calls us higher.

So don't isolate. Don't carry it all on your own. God didn't design you to be a one-man team.

Surround yourself with people who remind you that you're stronger, braver, and more loved than you think. That kind of team? It's not just about winning games. It's about growing in grace and truth—together.

You're not alone. And you never have to be.

Reflection Questions

1. Who's in your corner right now? How can you build or strengthen relationships with people who will help grow your faith?

2. Where in your life do you need to better balance quiet time with God and time spent in community?

— Coach Diso

91

He is Near

"The Lord is near to the brokenhearted and saves the crushed in spirit." — Psalm 34:18

We are wired to seek comfort in the presence of those who support us the most. I remember exactly where I was when I got the call that my dad had passed away suddenly. My world stopped. My family, friends, and FCA community surrounded me in those first few days. My teammates didn't just offer words—they showed up. They sat with me, prayed with me, and reminded me I wasn't walking through the pain alone. Their presence was a gift—proof that I was loved.

But as the days passed and life resumed, the crowd grew quieter. I found myself alone. The silence was deafening. Except I wasn't really alone. In that quiet space, I felt Jesus whisper, *I am here.* He was as close as I allowed Him to be. I started talking to Him—not with fancy words, just honest ones. I prayed through the ache. I opened my Bible and let His promises steady me. I journaled when I didn't know what else to do. Those small practices helped me let Him in. And the more I leaned in, the more I realized: His presence never left.

Athletes understand this. Before every game, we huddle—locking arms, locking eyes, reminding each other that we're in this together. We huddle before a play, ensuring we're on the same page. And we huddle afterward—whether in victory or defeat. The huddle is a place of unity, strength, and reassurance.

No one stands alone.

Neither do we in life.

> **"Be strong and courageous. Do not be afraid or terrified because of them, for the Lord your God goes with you; He will never leave you nor forsake you." — Deuteronomy 31:6**

God never leaves the huddle. Even when it feels like everyone else has moved on, He is still near—waiting for us to lean in. The question isn't whether He's there; it's whether we're letting Him be close.

Reflection Question

When have you felt alone, and how did you experience God's presence in that moment? How can you lean into Him today if you struggle to feel His nearness?

Your Challenge

Today, take a moment to step into the huddle with Jesus. Talk to Him. Be honest about where you are. Let Him be near.

— Coach Dickinson

92

Where is Your Cornerstone?

"For no one can lay any foundation other than
the one already laid, which is Jesus Christ." — 1
Corinthians 3:11

What are you building your life on?

The **cornerstone** is the most important part of a building's
foundation in construction. If it's strong and set correctly, the
building stands firm. If it's weak or misaligned, the entire structure
is unstable. The Bible tells us that **Jesus is our true foundation**,
but the truth is many of us set our cornerstone on things that won't
last.

Maybe your cornerstone is **your talent**, but what happens when
an injury sidelines you? Perhaps it's **your relationships**, but
what happens when people let you down? Maybe it's **your success—your wins, accolades, your reputation**—but what happens when the cheers stop? If your cornerstone is anything oth-
er than Christ, it does not matter *if* your foundation will crack,
but *when*.

I learned this firsthand in Olympic lifting. Not many people knew how to teach the *clean and jerk* or the *snatch*, but I had Coach Byrd—a firefighter who volunteered twice a week to train us. He didn't just show us how to lift; he taught us the fundamentals—**proper technique, consistent discipline, and focused attention to detail.** It wasn't just about strength; it was about building the right habits. That kind of foundation didn't just improve my lifting—it shaped how I approached everything else.

It's the same with your spiritual life. **Prayer, reading Scripture, obedience, and accountability**—these are your technique drills. They may not look flashy, but they build the strength that holds when pressure comes.

Athletic success is a gift—it can glorify God—but it was never meant to be your cornerstone. Instead, let Christ be your firm foundation. Achievements may come and go, but He never will.

Life works the same way. Jesus said:

> **"Therefore, everyone who hears these words of mine and puts them into practice is like a wise man who built his house on the rock. The rain came down, the streams rose, and the winds blew and beat against that house; yet it did not fall, because it had its foundation on the rock." — Matthew 7:24-25**

If you build your life on shaky ground—your own strength, success, or approval from others—you'll crumble under pressure. But if your cornerstone is **Jesus**, your foundation will never fail, no matter what storms come your way.

Reflection Question

What are you building your life on? If not Jesus, will your foundation hold when life gets tough?

Action Step

Take a moment today to evaluate where your cornerstone is. If you realize you've built on something temporary, ask God to realign your foundation with Him.

— Coach Dickinson

93

Peace

"And the peace of God, which transcends all understanding, will guard your hearts and minds in Christ Jesus." — Philippians 4:7

Let's be honest—one mistake can mess with your head.

Maybe you dropped the ball. Missed the shot. Blew the play. Or maybe it wasn't even on the field—maybe it was something you said or something you didn't do. Either way, it's like quicksand. The more you replay it in your mind, the deeper you sink.

I've coached a lot of athletes through that feeling. The doubt. The shame. The "Did I just ruin everything?" moments. And here's the truth I always come back to: **you're responsible for protecting your peace.** No coach, teammate, or circumstance controls it—only you—and the One who offers it freely: **Jesus.**

See, Jesus didn't leave us to figure this out alone. He set us up with everything we need to live in peace—real peace—not the fake kind that disappears when things go wrong. Here's how He did it:

1. The Holy Spirit Has Your Back

Jesus gave us the Holy Spirit—our daily guide and comforter. That means you're never actually facing anything alone. When you feel overwhelmed, He's right there, steadying you.

2. You're One with Jesus

Your mistakes don't define you. Your identity is locked in through your relationship with Christ. You're not some flawed athlete trying to earn worth—you're a child of God, already loved, already chosen. That changes the game.

3. He Gave Us a Playbook

The Word of God isn't just a book—it's the ultimate game plan for life. When you follow it, you're building on a solid foundation. You stop guessing, and you start walking with confidence.

4. He Calls Us to Love, Not Live in Regret

When we lead with love—for God, for others, and for ourselves—we silence shame. Love changes our focus. It reminds us that we're here to serve, encourage, and grow—not to be perfect.

5. He Gave Us Peace—Even in the Storm

Jesus didn't promise an easy life, but He *did* promise peace. And that peace doesn't always make sense to the world, but it will guard your heart when life gets loud.

So take a second. What's keeping you up at night? What regret are you still carrying? What fear is replaying in your mind like a highlight reel gone wrong?

Those things? They don't get to own you anymore.

Let Jesus take the weight. Don't let regret become your idol—something you keep bowing to. Regret is a terrible god. It offers no redemption, hope, or resurrection—only shame and self-condemnation. It binds you to the past and blinds you to God's grace in the present.

Give it to God. Fully. Freely. And watch how peace rushes in when you finally let go.

You can't change the past—but with Jesus in your corner, your future's wide open.

Breathe deep. Walk tall. You've got peace on your side.

Reflection Questions

1. What fears, regrets, or past mistakes steal your peace right now?

2. How can you shift your focus from negativity to love—and invite Jesus to lead you through it?

— Coach Diso

94

Have You Been Through Hell?

"They will be punished with everlasting destruction and shut out from the presence of the Lord and from the glory of his might." — 2 Thessalonians 1:9

If you played football, you probably remember two-a-days. Those grueling summer practices, where the heat was unbearable, your legs felt like concrete, and the coaches pushed you harder than you thought possible. At my school, we called it Hell Week. And if you've ever run gassers in the August sun in Florida, you might have thought, Yep, this must be what hell feels like.

Growing up, I also heard plenty of country songs about "going through hell." They painted pictures of tough times, heartbreak, and hard roads. And while those struggles were real, here's the truth: none of us have actually been to hell.

During those practices, we weren't alone. Our coaches were right there, pushing us, encouraging us, wanting us to succeed. Our parents and friends cheered us on from the sidelines, supporting us through every grueling drill. And even if someone didn't have family or friends in their corner, one presence still never left—God's love.

The reality is that no human has ever experienced hell—because no one has ever been completely separated from God. Psalm 139 reminds us that we can go nowhere to escape His presence: *"If I make my bed in Sheol, You are there"* (v. 8). Even in our darkest moments, He is near.

Hell isn't primarily about fire or torment—it's about **total separation** from God. That's what makes it terrifying.

God is love (1 John 4:8). God is peace (Philippians 4:7). God is light (John 8:12). Everything good, every bit of comfort or clarity your soul longs for, comes from Him. Hell is the absence of all of that.

No encouragement. No second chances. No love. No hope.

Even those who reject God still receive glimpses of His goodness—the laughter of teammates, the beauty of a sunset, or the strength to endure pain. But **hell is where all of that is gone**—not because God stops loving, but because He gives people the dignity of their decisions. Free will means God won't force Himself on anyone.

And often, it's in our deepest athletic or personal struggles—those two-a-days, those losses, those injuries—that we finally start reaching for Him. Trials break pride. Pain invites surrender. And in that desperation, we often find the nearness of God more clearly than ever before.

So, no, two-a-days weren't hell. That breakup wasn't hell. That job loss, that injury, that struggle—none of it was hell. Hard? Yes. Painful? Absolutely. But God was still there.

And if God is still with you, then there is still hope.

And as Paul states in Romans 8:31, *"If God is for us, who can be against us?"*

As long as you're still here, He's still calling you. The real question isn't "Have you been through hell?"—it's "Do you know the One who can keep you from it?"

Reflection Question

Have you ever walked through a difficult time and later realized God was with you the whole way? How does knowing He never leaves you change the way you face trials?

— Coach Dickinson

95

Chosen

"You did not choose me, but I chose you and appointed you." — John 15:16

If you've ever been in a locker room before a big game, you know what it feels like when the air shifts. Everyone's locked in. The coach steps up—and then—boom—a speech that hits you right in the soul. I've given a few of those and heard a few that still stick with me today. A good pregame speech doesn't just get you hyped to win—it reminds you *why you're* out there in the first place.

But here's the thing: sometimes, the motivation we really need isn't for a game. It's for life. And no matter how many speeches we've heard, there's one truth that trumps them all: **God picked you.** God knew you before you made your first tackle, ran your first lap, or even took your first breath. He knew what fires you up, what scares you, where you'd struggle, and where you'd shine. He handcrafted you for a purpose only you can fulfill. That should light a fire in your chest.

You're not some random player on a roster—you were *chosen*. And not just for this season or this team, but for something eternal.

God's been paying attention to every moment of your life. The wins, the losses, the injuries, the doubts, the dreams—He sees it all. And through it all, He hasn't taken His eyes off you.

There will be times when you feel like you're not enough. Like you don't have what it takes. That's when you need to hear God's voice louder than your doubts. He's the Coach who never misses a moment. Even while you sleep, He's watching over you. His plan for your life isn't small, and it's never by accident. You were made for more than stats or standings. You were made to know Him, to walk with Him, and to lead others to do the same. And you weren't meant to walk that path alone. Teams aren't just about plays and performance—they're about people. We were created to lift each other up, remind each other of what's true, pray when someone's hurting, and celebrate when someone is growing. That's what real teams do—they reflect the heart of God.

Jesus didn't just save you—He *appointed* you. That means He gave you a role to play, a mission, a calling that matters. You were built to carry something important into this world: love, strength, kindness, leadership, and truth. And even when you feel off your game, remember—your value isn't based on performance. It's based on who *chose* you.

So when life hits hard—when you feel disconnected, defeated, or unsure of your worth—go back to the basics: You are chosen. You are loved. You have a purpose.

Just like a great pregame speech fires up a team to leave it all on the field, God's Word fuels us to live with courage and confidence. You're not just playing for a moment—you're living for something bigger.

So suit up, take the field, and live like someone who was hand-picked by the Creator of the universe—because you were.

Reflection Questions

1. How do pregame speeches in sports relate to the broader theme of motivation and purpose in life?

2. How can your trust in God help you overcome feelings of doubt and insecurity?

— Coach Diso

96

God Collects Tears

"You keep track of all my sorrows. You have collected all my tears in your bottle. You have recorded each one in your book." — Psalm 56:8 (NLT)

There are moments in competition when the weight of the game, the season, or even life becomes overwhelming. You put in the work, sacrifice, and fight with everything you've got—only to fall short. Maybe it's an injury that takes you out, a heartbreaking loss in the final seconds, or the frustration of feeling unseen and unappreciated despite your effort. In those moments, it's easy to wonder: *Does any of this even matter?*

But some losses hit much harder than anything on the field or court. The kind that changes everything. Losing a loved one—a mother, a father, a grandparent—leaves a void that no championship, no victory, no amount of success can fill. Grief comes in waves. Some days, you push through just fine. Other days, a memory, a song, or even a familiar scent pulls you right back, and suddenly, the tears come.

I remember when my father died suddenly. At first, I tried to stay strong. I told myself I had to hold it together to keep moving forward. But then, it hit me. The weight of his absence, the finality of it all—I lost it. I broke down and cried. At that moment, I realized something: grief isn't a weakness. Tears aren't a failure. They are proof of love.

David, the writer of Psalm 56, knew what it was like to feel over-whelmed. He was on the run, fearing for his life, yet he clung to one truth—God saw him. Not only did God see him, but He kept track of his sorrows. The Lord collected every tear David shed, recorded, and remembered.

Athletes know the grind—the early morning workouts, the late-night film study, the countless hours refining their craft. The work is often unseen, but that doesn't mean it's forgotten. And neither are you. Just as a coach keeps track of stats, plays, and progress, God keeps track of every tear, every struggle, and every moment of pain you endure. Not one goes unnoticed.

But here's the most powerful part—God doesn't just collect tears; He redeems them. The pain you feel now will not be wasted. God is working through it, shaping you, strengthening you, refining you into the leader, the teammate, and the person He created you to be.

If you've lost someone close, know God sees your pain. He doesn't just acknowledge it—He holds it. Every tear shed in grief is sacred to Him. And while the hurt may never fully go away, He promises that one day, He will wipe every tear from your eyes (Revelation 21:4). That means no more sorrow, no more death, no more sepa-ration. Until that day, trust that He is walking with you through the grief, collecting every tear, and carrying you through.

Grief isn't something you have to carry alone. On a strong team, the others rally when one player is hurting. These small acts matter whether it's a moment of silence before a game, wearing a patch in someone's honor, or just sitting quietly beside a grieving teammate. God often uses your teammates to help carry your burden. And just as He collects your tears, He also redeems them—bringing comfort through community, healing through time, and purpose through the pain.

So, remember, when the tears come—whether from exhaustion, frustration, or heartbreak—God collects them. He sees you. He cares. And He will bring beauty from the struggle.

That truth stayed with me. It eventually became the foundation for my book, *Every Tear Remembered: God's Presence in Our Grief*. It reflects on loss, faith, and how God meets us in our pain. If this devotion resonates with you, I hope it encourages you to keep pressing into that hope.

Reflection Question

How does knowing that God collects your tears change how you handle setbacks, grief, and struggles?

— Coach Dickinson

97

Fully Equiped

"By his divine power, God has given us everything we need for living a Godly life." — 2 Peter 1:3

If you've ever worked with a personal trainer, you know they bring the plan—the drills, the knowledge, the steps to get stronger, faster, better. But here's the deal: it only works if you trust the process. You can't just go through the motions and expect championship results. I've seen athletes get stuck—not because the trainer wasn't legit, but because they didn't buy in. They didn't align their learning with what their coach was expecting.

And that? That's exactly what we do with God sometimes.

We try to push through life, grinding it out on our own strength, thinking hustle is enough. But the truth is—we already have access to *everything* we need to live the life God's called us to. He's not holding out on us. The moment we said "yes" to Jesus, we were handed the ultimate training plan, the perfect Coach, and the power of the Holy Spirit.

You can't ignore the Word, skip the reps in prayer, and still expect to be spiritually strong. Reps matter. Skipping the reps in prayer is like skipping practice—you miss the chance to grow. Growth doesn't come from coasting—it comes from commitment.

Spiritual transformation isn't something we muscle through. It's what happens when we let Jesus take the lead—when we trust Him, listen to Him, and lean into His plan instead of our own. That's where the real change happens. Not just getting better but becoming new. And just like a trainer never expects you to hit a max bench press on day one, God doesn't expect perfection. He *equips* you along the way. His power backs every step of obedience. Every challenge comes with His presence. He trains us not just to succeed—but to shine for His glory.

So whatever you're facing, whatever's in front of you—know this: **God has already given you what you need.** Now, it's on you to trust Him and step into it. Let's get after it.

Reflection Questions

1. In what areas of your life have you relied on your efforts instead of trusting in God's power and guidance?

2. What steps can you take to strengthen your relationship with Jesus?

— Coach Diso

98

Nothing Compares to His Promise

"For no matter how many promises God has made, they are 'Yes' in Christ. And so through Him, the 'Amen' is spoken by us to the glory of God." — 2 Corinthians 1:20

The world has much to say about who you are, what you can do, and what you're worth. If you listen long enough, you'll hear things like:

• "You're not good enough."

• "You'll never make it."

• "You don't have what it takes."

• "You're too weak. Too slow. Too broken."

The world tries to define you with limitations, labels, and lies. But God's voice speaks the Truth:

• "I have a plan for your life." — "'For I know the plans I have for you,' declares the Lord, 'plans to prosper you and not to harm you, plans to give you hope and a future.'" (Jeremiah 29:11)

• "Your life is no accident." — "Before I formed you in the womb I knew you, before you were born I set you apart." (Jeremiah 1:5)

• "Your life matters." — "You are the light of the world. A city set on a hill cannot be hidden." (Matthew 5:14)

• "I am always working on your behalf to bring you closer to Me." — "And we know that in all things God works for the good of those who love Him, who have been called according to His purpose." — Romans 8:28

God says:

• "You are fearfully and wonderfully made." — Psalm 139:14

• "My grace is sufficient for you, for My power is made perfect in weakness." — 2 Corinthians 12:9

• "You can do all things through Christ who strengthens you." — Philippians 4:13

• "I have called you by name. You are Mine." — Isaiah 43:1

God's promises don't shift with culture, feelings, or circumstances. They are unchanging, unshakable, and always true. The world's voice may be loud, but it will never be right.

Athletic competition puts all of this to the test. In one game, you're a hero; in the next, you're benched. Coaches yell, critics talk, and teammates sometimes echo the world's lies. But God's promises don't depend on your performance but on His character. That's why it's so crucial for teammates to speak the truth over one another. When someone's confidence is shaken, we remind them who they are in Christ. When the pressure hits, we lean on the consistency of God's Word, not the scoreboard.

One afternoon, I was listening to a kids' worship song with my daughter—*Shout to the Lord*, sung by a children's praise choir. As the music built, voices rose in joyful praise. Then, cutting through the chorus, a single whisper from a little girl echoed:

"Nothing compares to His promise."

That whisper hit harder than any cheer or shout. It reminded me that the most powerful truths often come quietly—and that God's promises speak louder than the world ever could.

"Nothing compares to His promise."

Her quiet voice was stronger than every doubt, fear, or lie the world tries to tell us. It reminded us that sometimes truth isn't found in the loudest voices but in the still, small ones that carry the weight of eternity.

So the next time doubt creeps in, when you feel like you're falling short, or when the world tries to define you—remember who God says you are. His promises are not just better; they are unshakable, eternal, and always true.

Nothing compares to them.

Reflection Question

What voices have you been listening to lately? How can you replace them with the promises of God today?

— Coach Dickinson

99

Generational

"Let us not become weary in doing good, for at the proper time we will reap a harvest if we do not give up." — Galatians 6:9

Graduation day hits differently when you've poured your heart into high school sports. For some, it's just another ceremony. For me, it was the closing chapter of a wild ride as a student-athlete—and the first page of something new. I stood in my cap and gown, thinking about the wins, losses, and people. One person who stood out big time was Coach Dickinson.

That day, he handed me a Bible with my name on it. Now, I'd gotten Bibles before—FCA camps, retreats, all that. But this one felt different. It wasn't a souvenir. It was a symbol. Coach believed in me—not just the athlete, but the man I could become. He was planting a seed he might never see grow.

Fast forward nearly 30 years, and guess what? That Bible is the only one I've kept. It's been with me through prayers, doubts, praises, and setbacks. The pages are worn but filled with memories, lessons, and raw moments of faith. When my son was heading off to boot camp for West Point, he was allowed to bring one thing: a Bible. I didn't even think twice. I handed him mine—Coach Dickinson's gift to me.

At the time, I figured it was just a practical choice. But then I got my son's first handwritten letter from boot camp. He wrote, *"Your Bible got me through it."* That hit me hard. One Bible, one coach, one act of faith—and now it had reached across generations.

A few months later, I was catching up with Coach Dickinson and told him the story. I wanted him to know just how far his kindness had stretched. He brushed it off with his usual humility, but I could see it landed. I needed him to know—he'd modeled perseverance, kindness, and quiet leadership. And now, I try to live those same values every day.

You never know who's watching. You never know what small gesture will echo through someone's or their kid's life. That's the beauty of what Jesus calls us to in Matthew 28:19: *Go and make disciples.* Keep doing good, even when it feels like no one sees because God sees. And at the right time, He brings the harvest.

Some of my old players have circled back, now mentoring the athletes I coach. That's full circle. That's legacy. And that's what this is all about.

One of my former players was quiet and steady and always showed up when he played for me. He didn't always lead with his voice, but he led with his consistency. Now he's coaching for me, speaking life into kids the same way I once spoke into him. Not because he had all the answers but because he saw what was possible when a coach believed in him. He is now creating his legacy with players, and that's the ripple effect of showing up.

So listen to your coaches, encourage your teammates, and be all-in all the time. You do not need to be perfect—you just need to be faithful. God will use your faithfulness in ways you can't even imagine. Jesus talked about this in His parable of the sower—how some seeds fall on good soil and grow strong, producing a harvest. When we invest in others with faith and love, we plant seeds in hearts ready to grow.

Because here's the truth: when we plant seeds with hope, courage, and conviction, God waters them with purpose. And those seeds? They grow into something generational.

Reflection Questions

1. What gift have you received that influenced and impacted your life?

2. In what ways can you apply the lessons of perseverance, kindness, and leadership to your own life—and how might those actions impact others in ways you may not immediately see?

— Coach Diso

100

Full Circle

"Let us run with perseverance the race marked out for us, fixing our eyes on Jesus, the pioneer and perfecter of our faith." — Hebrews 12:1–2

Coach Diso: Pause for a moment. Look back. You've made it through 100 devotions. That's not a small thing—it's 100 intentional steps toward growth, truth, and purpose. That's a season of showing up, not just to a book, but to the call God has placed on your life.

The race isn't just about the starting line or even the strides you've taken so far. Hebrews reminds us to fix our eyes on Jesus, who calls us forward. That focus will be your strength as you step into what's next.

This journey wasn't just checking boxes—it was about preparing your heart to lead, serve, and become the kind of athlete who walks with integrity, courage, and faith.

Coach Dickinson: We called this book *Pregame* for a reason. Everything you've read, every story, every Scripture—it's been about building your foundation. Like before any big game, you've stretched your faith, warmed your mind, and laced up with truth. But this? This is still just the beginning.

Along the way, you've dug into truth—about who you are, who God is, and how to live with perseverance, peace, and purpose. You've wrestled with identity, trust, humility, discipline, and the Fruits of the Spirit. You've been equipped not just with knowledge but with the kind of spiritual grit it takes to lead well and finish strong.

Pregame is preparation. Game Time is where it all gets tested. When you walk into the weight room, the locker room, the classroom—or face pressure in the real world—this is where faith turns into action. This is where truth gets legs and starts to move.

Coach Diso: You've been challenged to trust when things didn't make sense. You've been reminded that your worth doesn't come from stats or trophies. You've heard stories of real people walking through pain, doubt, and triumph—and choosing to keep going. You've learned that peace is possible, humility is powerful, and you're never alone on this journey.

Coach Dickinson: And now, the question becomes: what will you do with all of it? What's God calling you to step into next? How will you live this out—not just at practice, but in the locker room, the classroom, home, and wherever life takes you?

This next part—*Game Time*—isn't about more reading. It's about action.

It's time to live boldly. Lead with love. Play with purpose.

Coach Diso: You're ready. You've put in the work.

But remember, even now, you don't go alone. You've got team-mates. You've got us. And most importantly—you've got a Savior running the race with you every step of the way.

Let's go.

Coach Dickinson: *Pregame* may be over, but the mission is just getting started.

We'll see you in *FULL CIRCLE 360: A Devotional for Athletes—Game Time.*

Lord,

Thank You for this season of preparation. We give You praise for every word, challenge, and truth You planted in the heart of this athlete.

We pray that everything learned in this book will take root and grow bold.

When doubt creeps in, remind them of who they are.

When fear whispers lies, let Your voice be louder.

Give them the courage to live out their faith with fire and humility.

May they lead with love, compete with integrity, and walk in pur-pose—

not for their own glory but for Yours.

This is Your team, and we're ready.

In Jesus' name, Amen.

— Coach Dickinson & Coach Diso

About the Authors

COACH ANTHONY "DISO" PARADISO

Coach Anthony "Diso" Paradiso is a devoted coach, husband, and father. He and his wife, Jessica—an educator and coach—have been blessed with five children. Their son is a Cadet at the United States Military Academy at West Point, their three middle daughters are active in cheerleading, and their youngest daughter brings joy and energy to the heart of the family.

During high school, Coach Diso served as President of the Fellowship of Christian Athletes (FCA) while excelling as a multi-sport athlete in football, basketball, baseball, weightlifting, and track. His commitment to faith and mentorship carried into his coaching career, where he has served as an FCA Huddle Coach, camp leader, and community speaker—always championing his philosophy of *"Relationships over Results."*

Coach Diso's nearly 30-year career as a coach and educator in the public school system has spanned football, boys' and girls' weightlifting, basketball, baseball, track, girls' flag football, and Special Olympics. He is a proud member of Florida's prestigious 100-win club for high school football and is the only coach in the state's history to mentor two quarterbacks who each surpassed 10,000 passing yards and 100 touchdowns. He also developed a record-setting offense and has helped countless athletes reach their dream of playing at the collegiate level.

Throughout his journey, God has placed many mentors in his life—including Coach Christian A. Dickinson, with whom he has built a lifelong friendship. Three decades after their first meeting, their relationship has come full circle with the co-authorship of *Full Circle 360 Series: A Day Devotional for Athletes*—a testament to the power of faith, perseverance, and purpose-driven mentorship.

Still residing in Florida, Coach Diso actively coaches and mentors student-athletes. His personal experiences as an individual, athlete, and coach, paired with his heart for discipleship and building meaningful relationships, continue to inspire his mission of serving others through sports and faith.

FULL CIRCLE

A 360-DAY DEVOTIONAL FOR ATHLETES

COACH CHRISTIAN A. DICKINSON

 **Coach Christian A. Dickinson** is a husband, father, educator, coach, speaker, and leader passionate about mentorship and resilience. Married with four children, his life is as active off the field as on. His family reflects a love of sports and adventure, from extreme sports and soccer to NCAA Division 1 volleyball and now golf.

A former high school FCA President, Coach Dickinson laid the foundation of his faith early, later continuing the legacy as an FCA Sponsor and coach. His athletic journey includes playing and coaching football, basketball, weightlifting, and golf. While serving as assistant principal at Nease High School, Dickinson had a front-row seat to Tim Tebow's rise—witnessing the championship season that helped launch a legendary career.

Dickinson has served as a teacher, coach, principal, and executive director in education across PRE K–12 public, virtual, and private schools. While working on his forthcoming leadership book, *It's Great to Be a Grenadier: 7 Lessons in Leadership*, he found himself drawn into a new story—one that became *FULL CIRCLE*. What began as research into past lessons evolved into a present-day devotional journey, reigniting old friendships and planting new seeds of faith through sports.

As co-author of *FULL CIRCLE 360 Series: A Devotional for Athletes*, Dickinson brings faith and sports together through stories, scripture, and personal reflection. *Pregame* marks a new chapter—reuniting with Coach Anthony "Diso" Paradiso and Coach Neff after three decades to encourage the next generation of athletes.

He is the President and CEO of Learning Engineered Publishing, where he leads the creation of children's books, parenting resources, financial literacy programs, and leadership guides that inspire families and future leaders. As a speaker, he continues to share messages of faith, leadership, and purpose with schools, teams, and organizations nationwide.

FULL CIRCLE

A 360-DAY DEVOTIONAL FOR ATHLETES

More Books from the Authors

I f you enjoyed *FULL CIRCLE: PREGAME*, you may also appreciate these Christ-centered resources:

Paradiso/Dickinson:
FULL CIRCLE: GAME TIME — A Devotional Series for Athletes
(coming soon)
The whistle's blown. It's time to suit up. *GAME TIME* builds on the foundation of *PREGAME*, challenging athletes to live out their faith in the heat of competition. With real stories, Scripture, and hard-earned wisdom, Coach Dickinson and Anthony "Diso" Paradiso call athletes to lead with courage, compete with integrity, and pursue Christ in every moment—on and off the field.

Anthony "Diso" Paradiso:
Relationships Over Results: Why Who You Lead Matters More Than What You Win *(coming soon)*
A compelling call to coaches and leaders to prioritize people over performance—because discipleship doesn't stop at the scoreboard.

Christian A. Dickinson:
Jesus Was Funnier Than You Think: Unlocking His Wit,
Wisdom, and Unexpected Humor
A fresh look at the wit and humor of Jesus Christ —
revealing the brilliant, joyful ways He taught truth
and disarmed pride.

The Prophetic Equation: Thirty Prophets. One Christ.
Zero Coincidence.
An exploration of how thirty prophetic voices
across centuries, kingdoms, and crises converge with
stunning precision in Jesus Christ — revealing that
Scripture is not random, but a masterpiece of divine
design.

Micah 6:8: A Prophetic Bridge to Jesus
A concise biblical commentary exploring how one
ancient verse points forward to the life and ministry
of Christ.

The Curse of Time: Time Began When Eternity Broke
A theological and personal exploration of time
as a consequence of sin—not a neutral part of
creation. Drawing from Scripture, Church Fathers,
and moments of divine encounter, this book challenges
the assumption that time was God's original design
and invites readers to rediscover the eternal now of
God's presence.

Every Tear Remembered: God's Presence in Our Grief
A reflection on sorrow, healing, and hope through
the lens of God's enduring love.

Roar of 'Ēzer: Reclaiming God's Vision for Women's Strength

From Eden's garden to the early church, God named women 'ēzer—rescuer, strength-bearer, equal partner in His image. This compelling biblical exploration invites women to rise, not as shadows but as co-laborers in God's kingdom. With Scripture, story, and a call to courage, *Roar of 'Ēzer* reveals that women were never meant to shrink. They were always meant to roar.

It's All or Nothing: How Jesus Raised the Standard from Tithing to Full Surrender

A biblical commentary challenging traditional views of tithing by exploring Jesus' call to radical, Spirit-led generosity.

www.ingramcontent.com/pod-product-compliance
Lightning Source LLC
Chambersburg PA
CBHW070910120626
46546CB00001B/203